# FARM TO FORK
## ALL ABOUT FOOD

PRAFUL C. VIN

BLOOMSBURY
LONDON • NEW DELHI • NEW YORK • SYDNEY

*First Published, 2013*



**BLOOMSBURY PUBLISHING INDIA PVT. LTD.**
London New Delhi New York Sydney

ISBN: 978-81-924302-7-0

Published by Bloomsbury Publishing India Pvt. Ltd.
VISHRUT Building, DDA Complex, Building No. 3, Pocket C-6 & 7
Vasant Kunj, New Delhi 110 070

Laser Typeset by FORTUNE GRAPHICS
WZ 911/2 Shankarlal Street, Naraina, New Delhi

Printed at Anvi Composers
1 DDA Market, Block A-1B, Pachim Vihar, New Delhi 110 063

# Book Comments

I had certain apprehensions when I was asked to give my comments on this book. I thought it would be too technical and I would not be able to appreciate and judge the contents properly. Surprisingly, once I started reading it, I found it so interesting that I finished reading it in almost one go. The author has given a lot of interesting information and data and explained scientific and technical matters in a simple language. This is for the first time that I have come across a book that deals with so many issues and different aspects of the food we are consuming. Unless one reads the book, one cannot get an idea of how challenging a task it is to provide food security, enjoyable and safe food to our ever increasing population.

**Subhash C. Kashyap**
*Eminent Constitutional Expert and*
*Former Secretary General of Lok Sabha*

I found this book to be a very fluid and easily comprehensible overview on food, the food industry, food science and technology. For anyone, with or without a foods background, who wants to know more, or for the first time about food, beyond the daily meals, this book would be highly recommended.

**Subham Ray**
*Head, Private Brands*
*Future Value Retail Ltd (Food Bazaar)*

I believe this is the first and only book which deals with all aspects of food we consume, in a simple non-technical manner. It becomes easy for the reader who is concerned, but has no single source to find out about foods that affect all of us. This book will therefore fill that void.

**Kisan Mehta**
*Former President – Coca Cola India & S.W Asia*
*Former President – All India Food Processors Association*

The book has information for everyone who wants to know about various aspects of foods. The book will serve the purpose for those who want to have general knowledge, technical information, and referral and thus will serve as a valuable tool for entrepreneurs, developers, teachers and students. For industry, it will be a useful guide in developing, formulating, manufacturing and quality assurance of contemporary food products and their marketing. For the lay public, it will answer many queries about the food they consume.

**Prafull D. Sheth**
*Former Executive Vice President & Member of the Board*
*Ranbaxy Laboratories Limited*
*Vice President*
*International Pharmaceutical Federation (FIP)*

*Dedicated to*
*the memory of my late parents*
*Manugauri & Chetanlal Vin*

# Foreword

The roots of civilization are based on the collaborative efforts for food production. For all nations, food security is of paramount importance. From a nearly starving nation at the time of independence in 1947, India today has emerged as one of the largest producers of food in the world. In fact, India as the second largest producer in the world has the potential of becoming the biggest in the world in the food and agriculture sector. At the same time, there is the ever changing scenario and many new challenges. No wonder, the five year plans laid heavy emphasis and priority on this sector.

At such a juncture, this book *'Farm to Fork – All About Food'* by our friend, Mr. Praful Vin is indeed timely. It is, perhaps the first book of its kind relating to food from production till consumption. It covers various aspects including preservation, varieties, perception of taste and flavour and practical aspects of production, quality and marketing. It is based on decades of experience of a keen observer and a dedicated technocrat.

In the years to come, there will be greater growth opportunities and many changes. The issues like sustainable agriculture, new demands for eco-friendly and organic farm inputs and startling developments in GM foods will be some key factors. Food security, employment and health of nations will depend on how well they organize *'Farm to Fork'* chains.

Our academic courses need to cover the various aspects brought out in this book. I am sure the book will be of much use to a large cross section of academia, practicing technologists, managers and planners. Since it is written in a simple and direct way of communication, it will also be a useful reference for housewives and hoteliers!

I am extremely happy to welcome *'Farm to Fork'* and congratulate the author for presenting his rich and versatile experience in such a lucid manner.

Baroda
*20 August, 2012*

**Padmashree Dr. M. H. Mehta**
*Chairman – The Science Ashram,*
*Gujarat Life Sciences, Baroda*
*Ex Vice Chancellor,*
*Gujarat Agricultural University*

# Appreciation

The enactment of the Food Safety and Standards Act 2006 was a milestone in modernizing the food processing industry in India. The Prevention of Food Adulteration Act 1954 had lost its relevance as India was moving from the Inspector Raj to market reforms based on good global practices. India realized that the laws need to be modernized and standards harmonized globally to protect the health and safety of its citizens. As a member of the Central Committee of Food Standards (CCFS), I found that there was a lot of mistrust that existed between the food industry and the regulatory bodies. Consumers were completely kept out of the loop while setting standards and there was hardly any initiative by any of the stakeholders to educate and empower the consumers on healthy food habits and choice based on safety and certification.

This book *'Fart to Fork: All About Food'* authored by Shri Praful C. Vin is timely and is an interesting publication for all the players in the food chain in India. It has, at one place provided comprehensive information about the various aspects of food from the stage of harvesting to the point of consumption by the consumer. I would cherish the idea of such publications translated in various Indian languages so that every citizen is able to access such information, which will provide an informed choice to the various stakeholders involved in the food supply chain in India.

As a member of the Food Safety and Standards Authority of India representing the consumer, my one point agenda has been to ensure that we have standards which protects the health and safety of the consumers and the information is disseminated in a manner that the consumers understand while purchasing food in a Mall or a small retail store, which exhibit a plethora of packaged foods in various shapes and sizes from all over the world. The challenge is to communicate truthfully to the consumers on the benefits of packaged foods and how consumers can access safe and healthy food at the most affordable costs. It has been observed globally that good manufacturing practices based on evidence based science have always made food very affordable and accessible to the consumers. We have to reduce wastage of food and misguided subsidies, which has made the quality food in India most unaffordable to the majority of consumers. I find the author has touched these issues appropriately in the book.

I would like to conclude by congratulating the author for such an excellent publication and appeal to the readers to educate the consumers on how our traditional food and eating habits have always enabled us to lead a healthy life. We all should protect and respect our rich culture and make the world learn from India on the art of food processing, preservation and supply and set best standards, which are India centric and in the interests of the Indian consumer.

New Delhi
*20 August 2012*

**Bejon Misra**
*Founder, Healthy You Foundation*
*www.bejonmisra.com*

# Preface

One day I realized the similarity between the food industry and the movie industry. Both are commercial activities. A lot of hard work is carried out before a movie is screened. Similarly, a lot of hard work needs to be done as well before a new food product is introduced in the market. Both industries require creativity, technical skills and an understanding of people's choices. The purpose of the movie industry is to appeal to the eyes and ears of the viewer, while that of the food industry is to appeal to the tongue and nose. Both industries have tremendous potential to do good or harm to the population at large – mentally by the movie industry and physically by the food industry. I believe our movie industry has changed a lot over time in terms of technology and content. The food industry has also started changing in a similar fashion. Whether the changes are for better or for worse, are open to debate.

After major changes in the economic policy of the country in the 1990s, business conditions started changing for most industries, and the food industry has been no exception. Today, if one were to visit a mall, the person would be amazed to see a wide array of new food products on the shelves in very attractive packing. These food products were not visible fifteen years ago. With so many options, the taste of India is changing. The young generation has readily accepted pizzas, burgers, pastas, noodles, ready to eat factory-packed snacks, soups, energy drinks, sodas, chocolates, cakes, pastries, etc. Another important change is that the number of working women has increased. As a result, their disposable income has gone up. They have lesser time now, more disposable income, and are therefore showing an increasing preference for good quality convenience foods. Health, convenience and taste are the new buzzwords in the food industry. Mothers want to give their children what they like, in terms of taste, while ensuring that the food is healthy. As a famous advertisement of Knorr soups says – 'Tummy bhi khush aur mummy bhi khush'.

Food habits and lifestyles are changing. In a competitive world, life is full of tensions and is stressful. Due to lack of time and various other factors, physical activities have reduced. As a result, the problem of obesity is rising, leading to diseases like diabetes and cardiovascular problems. Experts estimate that India will have the world's largest population of people with such diseases and other lifestyle-related diseases. If you need to protect yourself, it would be useful if you start knowing your foods.

There are multiple aspects related to foods, from production to consumption that warrant attention. The media does highlight some issues related to foods, but these appear in isolation. Therefore, I saw the need for a comprehensive book on the subject of food. I have made an attempt to cover almost all aspects of food in simple and lucid language, so that even an average reader can understand.

I hope readers will find this book informative, educative, interesting and beneficial.

Baroda
*1 August 2012*

**Praful C. Vin**

# Acknowledgements

I would like to thank Mr. Neeraj Haseeja of Ms Zydus Wellness – it was he who during one of my conversations with him suggested that I write a book on food for various professionals like him, who are linked to the food industry in one way or another, but were not well versed with the different aspects related to food. His suggestion set me thinking and thus began my long journey of writing this book.

I also thank my family members Jaideep and Meera for helping me with the typing of the manuscript and for their help with the huge amount of research that goes into writing such a book. My son, Jeet for his suggestions and critical inputs regarding the contents of this book. Finally, my wife Ketki for not only being my life partner, but for always being there in my long career spanning 45 years in the food industry.

# Contents

# 1

# Food and Mankind

Early man was a hunter and lived in caves. He learnt about food production around 10,000 B.C. He did so by tilling the soil using simple tools made of stone. He used wild varieties of edible plants and produced crops. India was one of the first countries to start food production on the banks of river Ganga. Among the other countries that started agricultural activities were Iran, Iraq, Israel and their adjoining areas. Over a period of time, agricultural activities spread to other parts of the world, and different countries developed different crops depending on their weather conditions, suitability of land, availability of water, etc. India first cultivated wheat, barley and spices. China produced beans and lentils. The Far East produced rice. The western hemisphere produced tomato, maize, potato, cocoa bean and tobacco. To protect and transport crops from the fields, animals like dogs, horses, donkeys and ponies were domesticated. Animals were also raised as livestock for use as food. It is reported that in 1492, a global exchange took place for crops and animals between countries of the old world and the new world.

Initially, people produced food for their own consumption. Gradually, more and more people started working in the fields and got involved in the activities in a collaborative manner. This resulted in the formation of villages and as time passed, settlements became bigger and bigger. The quantum of food production increased due to improved methods of production. People improved yields by using natural manures, better tools, etc. This resulted in surplus food, and as a result, people started trading activities to dispose off the surplus food. As technology and efficiencies improved, people working in the fields became surplus. According to anthropologists, people who became surplus from agriculture, turned to other activities, such as mechanization of agriculture, industrialization, construction, literature, etc. Simply put, food is at the root of the modern civilization. Also, as more and more varieties of food items became available, people developed the art of cooking. People developed recipes by blending various food items, adding seasonings, etc., and cooked them in utensils by using fire, or by frying, or in ovens. Historically, people gathered in groups to enjoy eating foods and to celebrate happy occasions. This holds true in most of the parts of the world. Over a period of time, people also developed the art of garnishing foods and serving them in special crockery, or in expensive metal plates made of silver, gold, etc.

Before human beings started producing food, the population of human beings was estimated to be less than 15 million. In about 12,000 years, we now have a population of about 6.5 billion people. Throughout this period, human beings kept on inventing ways and means to improve their quality of life. As a result, today there are a wide variety of foods not only for sustaining life, but also for enjoyment. The concept of restaurants is perhaps only a few centuries old. Even in a developing country like India, people are spending almost ₹ 43,000 crore on eating outside their homes. Eighty per cent of this money is spent in restaurants that are in the unorganized sector. Today, we have many foreign restaurant chains in India, and one can find various cuisines including Chinese, Mexican, Thai and Italian available in almost all cities. There are many positive aspects of human civilization, but there are an equal number of negative aspects too which are worrisome, and can have an impact on food security. Some selfish people, in trying to get richer have exploited natural resources without worrying about other people living in such areas, as well as future generations. This has led to serious environment-related problems all over the world. The issue of global warming is much talked about, and this could have a direct impact on the food security of several countries. Modern civilization has also created disparities amongst people. Today, in India and in many other countries, people are starving, or are undernourished.

As per a Food and Agriculture Organization (FAO) report, we have at least 925 million people the world over who are undernourished. Most of the 925 million undernourished people (62 per cent of the total) live in Asia and the Pacific region, the world's most populous region, followed by sub Saharan Africa which is home to 26 per cent of the world's undernourished population. In India, a staggering 43 per cent of children are underweight and 48 per cent of the underweight children's growth is stunted by malnutrition. India is a country where more than 50 per cent of the population makes its living from agriculture, as compared to the global average of 30 per cent. Also, it is surprising that exports of food items are more than the imports of agricultural produce. It is important to remember that India was one of the first countries to begin agriculture. It is also true that India is ranked as the second highest producer of agricultural produce.

The over exploitation of the resources of the earth is worrisome. As Mahatma Gandhi said, *'There is enough food to meet everyone's needs, but not everyone's greed.'* It appears that one day Gandhi will be proved right by modern civilization.

# 2

# Food Production and Processing

## FOOD PRODUCTION

The author was brought up in Ahmedabad and remembers having waited in long queues for getting rations when he was hardly 12 years old. Elder family members used to relieve him before his turn came. He also remembers the Guest Control Order in force at that time. According to the Order, there were restrictions regarding the number of guests who could be invited for occasions like weddings, religious ceremonies, etc. People always defied or circumvented the Order by inviting people in smaller groups, and also at different venues. For many years this situation continued, until a bold and considerate Minister of Food and Agriculture – Rafi Ahmed Kidwai lifted all the restrictions. Since then, staple food items such as wheat, rice, sugar, etc., are freely available in the market. Sometimes, they are in short supply, which leads to spikes in prices till additional supplies are organized by importing the item under question by the government. As such, there is no acute shortage, but even then almost 21 per cent of the population is undernourished. This is because they cannot afford the cost of staple food items. The government is supplying food items at concessional prices through PDS (Public Distribution System) to people below the poverty line. It is also heavily subsidizing inputs for farmers to bring down their costs of production, but the real solution is in improving the productivity, i.e. yield per acre in agriculture, and improving the marketing and distribution of agricultural produce.

The Public Distribution System appears to be an ideal solution on paper to provide enough food, but everyone knows about its shortcomings. This is due to heavy leakages in the system. There is a nexus between politicians, officers involved in procurement and distribution, and also the business community which deals in trading and in making of *atta* and other similar products. Even the late Rajiv Gandhi, when he was Prime Minister, stated that out of one rupee that the government spends for a poor man, only 15 paisa reaches him. In view of this situation, a new system of giving each citizen a Unique Identification Number and then transferring cash in his bank account is being implemented. There are doubts about the success of this new scheme also. It is feared that cash will not be spent on food, but on alcohol consumption, or for other undesirable purposes.

Price volatility depends on demand and supply, but in India shortages are created deliberately by hoarders and politicians. From time to time, prices of commodities like sugar, oils, onions, potatoes, etc., which are consumed by the ordinary people increase to a level that they become too expensive. Surprisingly, when a lot of hue and cry is raised when prices go up very high, the prices get restored back to normal in no time without any fresh supply being received. This indicates that such price rises happen only due to the vested interests of powerful people and traders. Government is procuring almost 65 million tonnes of cereal and maintains this stock for handling such crisis, but wittingly/unwittingly the stock is not released in time, or supplies do not reach in time, especially in remote areas.

It is interesting to know that India supports 18 per cent of the world's population but with only two per cent of the total land mass. It is the second highest producer of agro products. Some of the production figures for 2009 for the top 20 most important commodities produced in India are listed in Table 2.1.

**Table 2.1:** Annual Production of Certain Commodities in India for 2009

(Courtesy: FAOSTAT, FAO Website)

| *Commodity* | *Annual Production (in metric tonnes)* |
|---|---|
| Sugarcane | 285029000 |
| Rice, Paddy | 133700000 |
| Wheat | 80680000 |
| Buffalo Milk, Whole, Fresh | 62860000 |
| Cow Milk, Whole, Fresh | 45140000 |
| Potatoes | 34391000 |
| Vegetables Fresh, NES** | 28006300 |
| Bananas | 26996600 |
| Maize | 16680000 |
| Onions, dry | 13900000 |
| Mangoes, Mangosteens, Guavas | 13557100 |
| Tomatoes | 11148800 |
| Eggplants | 10377600 |
| Coconuts | 10148000 |
| Soybeans | 10050000 |
| Cassava | 9623000 |
| Millet | 8810000 |
| Cottonseed | 8138000 |
| Fresh Fruit, NES** | 7983900 |
| Sorghum | 7250000 |

** NES means Not Elsewhere Specified

Today, approximately 400 grams of cereals are available per capita per day.

For providing adequate food, security experts believe that agricultural output must grow at the rate of 4 per cent per year against the current rate of 2.7 per cent. In order to achieve this kind of growth, agricultural reforms are necessary. Even though this fact is known to politicians, they still don't want to go ahead with reforms as far as possible. Agricultural reforms would involve and also impact many people, and political parties are always worried about the negative political fallout of such measures.

Listed now are some of the problems which we are facing at present that affect agriculture and food production:

1. There is a high rate of illiteracy amongst farmers and as a result, they have many limitations.
2. Most of them are marginal farmers and they have landholdings of less than 5.0 acres. In the USA the average landholding of farmers is 434 acres.
3. Farmers are always dependant on local financiers who exploit them. Our nationalized banks have opened branches in rural areas to provide finance but in situations when there is crop failure, the farmers are always under pressure by recovery agents. As a result, several farmers commit suicide. Many times amnesty schemes are offered, but they are too little and too late.
4. Most farmers are dependent on monsoon rainfall. Almost 60 per cent farmers are dependent on rains. In case of low rainfall, where irrigation is possible, they are able to save their crop, but they are helpless in case of too much rain.
5. There are so many areas in Assam, Bihar, West Bengal, etc., where rivers overflow every year and floods do a lot of damage to standing crops. Also in case of shortage of water, disputes between states about water sharing is always a political conflict. For many years now, the Central government has been talking of creating a water grid by drawing water from different rivers which can solve problems of flooding as well as shortages of water.

Obviously, such a massive project will involve displacement of thousands of farmers in many states, and this could become a serious political problem for ruling governments in many states. The completion of the Narmada river dam in Gujarat took several years, but now after its completion, people are able to see the benefits. Gujarat has attained 11 per cent growth in agriculture and has also helped industries to meet their water requirements.

As reported by FAO, the share in total water use in agriculture is 90.4 per cent, industry 2.2 per cent and domestic 7.4 per cent. As industrialization grows, demand for water by industries will grow significantly. Currently, farmers are pumping more water than they require due to cheap or free electricity available to them, and this has resulted in lowering of the ground water levels. Management of water resources will assume great importance in the not too distant future. Progressive farmers have already started drip irrigation.

6. Farmers are deprived of proper marketing services. There are now APMC's (Agricultural Produce Marketing Committees) which have come up in district headquarters, but small farmers are not able to market their produce directly. There are always four to five intermediaries involved before a small farmer's produce reaches the consumer. In India, a farmer gets only 20 to 25 per cent of the price paid by the consumer. In other countries the figure is almost 50 per cent. It is believed that if we have multi-product retail chains in the country, such as Walmart, it would benefit both the farmers and the consumers. These chains have extensive knowledge in creating front and back end infrastructure and supply chains for marketing of foods. They have the resources and experience of marketing agricultural produce. There have been a lot of debates and discussions about giving them entry, but they have not been able to gain entry as yet. It is worthy to note that their entries into countries

like China, Thailand, etc., have benefitted the farmers in those countries. The main objection to their entry is the likely impact on small businessmen in the retail sectors, but they are known to create more jobs in their operations than the number of people who could be out of business.

7. Small farmers have limitations of finance, plot size, education, etc., and are not in a position to adopt modern methods of agriculture. Due to ignorance, they use excessive amounts of fertilizers and pesticides which affects the fertility of the land and health of the people. About four decades ago, India had the green revolution with the help of the USA by using synthetic fertilizers and pesticides. Till today, their use is heavily subsidized, but now some rethinking is necessary.

Rethinking is also required for storage of farm produce. Almost 10 per cent of the produce of cereals is wasted due to problem of rodents and animals in the fields, and due to improper storage, which many a time is done even in open areas. Rotting of millions of tonnes of cereals is shown by the electronic and print media which have drawn the attention not only of citizens, but also of the Supreme Court. For safe preservation, grains need to be stored in silos, but due to some reasons they are stored in godowns and in the open.

In recent times, biological sciences have made rapid progress. In the early 1960s, two scientists, namely Watson and Crick were awarded the Nobel Prize for identifying and working out the chemical structure of the gene – the basic material in a living organism which is responsible for heredity and producing thousands of proteins for the functioning of a living system. This knowledge, and the subsequent work of other scientists including India born Nobel Prize winner Dr. Hargobind Khurana has led to modern inventions in biotechnology, genetics, etc., which has shown the new way for agriculture production. The crops produced by these methods are called GM crops meaning genetically modified crops. In these crops the seed containing the genes are modified, such that a specific change is introduced in the crop. The change could be to improve resistance to pests, herbicides, etc. More on this aspect is covered in the last chapter.

## PROCESSING OF FOODS

When there is value addition in a primary food, it is considered to be a processed food. In this sense, we were processing foods even before India got Independence. We had pulse mills, oil mills, rice mills, masala mills, etc., but the degree of processing was low. In the fifties, foods which involved a higher degree of processing were imported mostly from the UK, for the consumption of the elite. Locally made bread was sold at retail outlets of bakeries by wrapping it in old newspapers. Ice cream was not manufactured in factories, but was made using a hand operated *sancha* and served in loose glass or metal cups. Butter was sold as *maska*, wrapped in special paper known as butter paper. People were not aware about cheese and many thought *paneer* to be cheese. Typical Indian snacks and sweets were sold loose. Only some hard boiled candies, chocolates and biscuits were sold in a wrapped condition. Aerated drinks, mostly soda water and some flavoured drinks were sold in glass bottles, with marbles as closures. We have come a long way from this situation but the food industry is still in its infancy. To illustrate this point, we can consider the example of a very popular item like ice cream. In India, the consumption of ice cream per capita per year is only 300 ml, whereas in our neighbouring countries like Pakistan it is 700 ml and China 7000 ml. For other processed foods also, our consumption figures are quite low.

The Indian food processing industry is mainly in the unorganized sector. About 42 per cent is in the unorganized sector, 33 per cent in the small-scale sector and only 25 per cent is in the organized sector. Food processors in the unorganized sector are sometimes not registered, and small-scale units have less than rupees one crore as fixed assets. Because of this reason almost 75 per cent of the units are not able to afford upgradation of technology and are unable to employ qualified technical personnel to meet the stringent standards prescribed under the food laws. If new rules are rigidly implemented, many players will have to give up their businesses. Alternatively, corruption will rise. Companies in the organized sector are growing fast. In the case of the established categories of processed foods, demand is rising, and will continue to rise. This increase comes from both horizontal and vertical growth, i.e. increase in per capita consumption, and increase in the number of consumers. The demand for such products is far from the saturation point. In the meantime, newer categories of processed foods have started appearing in the market. Of course, success of new food products depends on many factors like consumer's likes, convenience and affordability.

Apart from these factors, there are several other factors such as the creation of awareness through extensive advertising and marketing, availability of the food item through a strong distribution network and the status of competition. As per available data, in 2004-05, the food processing sector contributed about 14 per cent of manufacturing GDP, contributing ₹ 2,80,000 crore. Of this, the unorganized sector accounted for more than 70 per cent of the production in terms of volume and 50 per cent in terms of value. This data includes processes such as grading, sorting and packaging, which enhance the shelf life of food products. The following data gives details of percentages of various types of processed foods:

**Table 2.2:** Percentage Production of Processed Foods
(Courtesy: D&B Research)

| | |
|---|---|
| Meat, Fish, Fruits, Vegetables and Oils | 40.2 per cent |
| Beverages | 19.6 per cent |
| Grain Mill Products | 10.8 per cent |
| Dairy Products | 5 per cent |
| Others | 24.5 per cent |

The data does not show the degree of processing or measures of value addition. The data includes simple processing such as grading, sorting, extraction of oils, grinding of grains, packaging, etc. Therefore, there is great scope for further value addition in terms of processing. For example, the dairy industry started out only by collection, chilling and transportation of milk over long distances in insulated vans. Gradually, products such as butter, milk powder, cheese, etc., which have much more value addition are now available and their demand is rising. Although dairy products only form 5.0 per cent of processed foods, they have made a significant contribution to the rural economy.

Today meat, fish and poultry products are available in a ready to cook state, and the demand will increase for ready to eat products. Already, several typical Indian products in ready to eat forms have come to the market, and many cooked meals are exported in a frozen form. The Ministry of Food Processing has taken policy initiatives to provide many incentives for promoting processed food industries. The Ministry is not only providing financial assistance, but is also going to create infrastructure that specifically caters to the needs of the food industry. They are going to create food parks and mega food parks, and will also develop integrated cold chain facilities, irradiation facilities, etc.

If one studies the history of multinational food companies, one would find that many of them had very modest beginnings. The founder of a company started operations in the backyard of his building. In India, many food companies had a very small operation. This is true across many categories of foods, such as snack foods, bakery products, soft drinks, ice creams, confectionery, etc. The success of these companies has one common factor, i.e. the founder's ability to identify the likes of the consumer, and offering the consumer an improved version of the product that he is used to.

As mentioned earlier, 70 per cent of the output of processed foods is in the unorganized sector, but as time progresses some of the small-scale (SSI) units will grow bigger into medium-scale or large-scale units. The main difficulty in growing for the small-scale units, is on the marketing front. Advertising and marketing of products has become extremely expensive. However, for companies that are able to offer good quality food products, the opportunities are increasing. The last five to six years have seen the growth of organized retail, also called the modern retail format. These retail chains have their own distribution channels. Small companies with good quality products now have the opportunity to market their products through the modern retail format, since they do not have to worry about having their own distribution network. They can hand over their products to the main warehouse of the retailer. More importantly, such companies can also supply to the big retailers under the retailer's brand name. These retail chains have started offering fast-moving consumer goods (FMCG) under their own labels, called private labels, or store brands. For example, retail chains like *More* (Aditya Birla Retail) and Big Bazaar, are marketing food products under their own brand name of *Feasters, Tasty Treat, Fresh* and *Pure*, etc. These products are not only as good as the leading FMCG brands, but are offered at prices that are 15-20 per cent lower than the leading brands available to consumers. This has been possible due to savings on advertisement expenses in the electronic and print media. Promotional activities are carried out in stores, by comparing them against branded established products. Private label arrangements have worked well in developed countries, and there is no reason why they would not work in India. Already, business newspapers have started reporting success stories of many food products. This arrangement has benefited small competent manufacturers, consumers and retail stores. Retail stores are benefitting, because they get higher margins than those offered by established brands. They are also not dictated terms by giant companies. Also, private labels are a good way for one retail chain to differentiate their offerings from the others. It has been reported that in the recent economic crises in the USA and other developed countries, demand for private label food products has increased. In fact, fear has been expressed by manufacturers of established branded products, that even after the economy recovers, some consumers will not return back to their brands.

There is already demand for customized processed foods by institutions. The defense services, state government agencies, railways, airlines, etc., require huge quantities of several products, and their demand will continue to grow. In addition to these institutions, large retail fast foods chains have come up in a big way. They too need standardized and customized products for their franchisees. In urban areas, large multi-specialty hospitals have come up, and they too require special purpose diet food items for their patients. Also, in public places and offices, vending machines for serving cold drinks and hot beverages have been provided.

There is little doubt, that with the passage of time, more and more women will start working, and they will not find much time to spend in the kitchen. But, they would not compromise with their duty of feeding family members with wholesome, healthy, tasty and yummy foods. In order to do this, they will need good quality processed foods that offer convenience, are not very time-consuming and reduce the efforts of cleaning kitchen utensils etc. In developed countries, the food industry has met the expectations of housewives, and India's food industry will also rise to meet the challenges.

It is obvious, that with the growth of the food industry, the packaging industry will also grow in equal measure. Also, demand for basic processing machinery and equipment such as reactor tanks, conveyors, heating equipment such as boilers, refrigeration machinery, vehicles for distribution, etc., will grow in a big way, as most food factories will need them, in addition to special purpose machinery and equipment, depending on the nature of food products.

The food industry will also require professionals, such as food technologists for quality control and research and development work, mechanical and electrical engineers for operation and maintenance of machinery and equipment, marketing and sales executives, accountants, etc. It will also provide employment to skilled and unskilled workers. To appreciate what the food industry can do, one should look at the growth of the dairy industry, and the prosperity it has brought to the rural economy by heralding a white revolution, and making India the world's largest milk producing nation. It was the vision of the late Sardar Vallabhbhai Patel, who was the son of a farmer, who suggested the setting up of a co-operative society of milk producers to market milk and milk products. Of course, the co-operative society was fortunate to have an able and exceptional leader supported by competent colleagues. There is no doubt, that there will be many similar success stories in the future as well, now that the Government of India has realized the importance of the food industry.

# 3

# Preservation by the Processing of Foods

To sustain life, the availability of food is of paramount importance. To ensure availability, food preservation is essential. The preservation of food dates back to antiquity, but as knowledge of microbiology and food chemistry grew, methods of preservation and processing improved. Modern food processing technology not only helps in preserving foods, but also converts them into a form that is enjoyable, and can be transported over long distances. Processed foods can be fortified with nutrients, and they are also convenient and save preparation and cooking time. Food-processing provides a link between the food producers and food consumers. As a result, the food processing industry plays a vital role in the economy of a nation. Industrialization of present group of developed countries was based on sound foundations laid down by the food-processing industry.

Of course, all such products must be properly packed, and should have a shelf life which is long enough for consumption. When foods are processed, issues arise of safety and changes in the composition of foods. To overcome problems of safety, Good Manufacturing Practices (GMP) and sanitation procedures need to be followed. To take care of changes in composition, functional food additives are required. Their role is discussed in the next chapter.

## TRADITIONAL WAY OF FOOD PRESERVATION

A long time ago, people observed that food items when dried under the sun remained consumable, though the taste and appearance changed. They did not know how sun drying helped, but they used this method for agro commodities like cereals, fruits and vegetables, etc. Even housewives found that when certain food preparations without cooking were sun dried, they could use such items for quite some time. Today, the most common and popular snack *papad* is a sun dried item. Many housewives make potato chips, banana chips, *aam papad, aamchur, papadi* made out of rice, sago, etc., by sun drying. Housewives also found that deep fat-fried products could also be consumed for longer times. During frying the moisture gets replaced by oil. Today, we know that in all these cases, moisture is removed from the food items, which is required by microbes to grow.

People also observed that food items when covered by a sugar or salt solution, remained consumable. Today, housewives are making jams at home, by using a highly concentrated sugar solution. In sugar syrup, the dissolved sugar creates an osmotic pressure which resists microbes. Pickles made at home are covered with edible oil. The oil is free from moisture, and microbes cannot grow and spoil the material which is covered below the surface of the oil. In pickles, acids such as vinegar and lactic acid, etc., are used, which make conditions unfavourable for microbes. At present, health authorities the world over have permitted the use of chemicals like sodium benzoate and sulphur dioxide which are very effective and harmless. They are categorized as Class II preservatives. In the Class I list, natural and traditionally used preservatives are included.

## CURRENT METHODS OF FOOD PRESERVATION

Living micro-organisms (bacteria, yeast, mold, virus, etc.) require water, food and favourable temperatures for their survival and multiplication. They therefore compete for foods that we consume.

The basic principle of food preservation is to render food in a form which cannot be consumed by micro-organisms. Alternately, the micro-organisms should be eliminated. The problem of protection from invasion by insects and other higher forms of life, is taken care of, at the food production level, by using insecticides, pesticides and fumigants before processing. Insecticides and pesticides are chemicals which prevent attacks by insects and pests. Fumigants are in gas form, and they destroy living insects, weevils, their eggs, etc., in cereals and other foods.

The various principles of protecting foods from micro-organisms which are currently used are as follows:

**Dehydration:** Is removal of moisture or water from food, since microbes in the absence of water cannot multiply.

**Sterilization/Aseptic Packing**: Food is packed in airtight containers and subjected to high temperatures to kill micro-organisms present in the food. In the case of aseptic packing, food is sterilized separately, and transferred to a sterile container in such a way that microbes cannot enter the food in the container while being transferred, or after packing.

**Refrigeration**: Storing foods at low temperatures so that microbes cannot grow due to unfavourable temperature conditions.

The machinery and equipment to process foods are designed based on these principles. A brief idea about them is given in the following paragraphs.

### Dehydration

In the past and also presently, in many cases, sun drying is used for the purposes of dehydration. Modern technology is very advanced, and there are different types of equipment used, depending on the composition of the food, state of food (solid or liquid), quality of the end product required, speed of drying required, energy costs involved, etc. Essentially they are designed to work on three principles, namely:

1. *Surface heating of foods*: The heat converts the moisture into water vapour which then escapes from the food through various pores.
2. *Passing or bubbling of dry, hot air through foods*: In this case dry, hot air absorbs moisture from the food making it dry.
3. *Removal of moisture from foods directly from the solid phase (ice) to the gaseous state (vapour)*: Water in a liquid state does not come into the picture during the process of drying.

Tunnel drier, tray drier, drum drier are examples of equipment based on the principle of surface heating of foods. Bakery products such as biscuits, cakes, bread, breakfast cereals and snack foods are examples of food made using such equipment.

Fluid bed drier, spray drier, hot air oven are examples of equipment using hot air for drying of foods. Powder products such as milk powder, vegetable and fruit powder are produced using such equipment.

Freeze driers are used in which foods are frozen before drying, and then they are subjected to a high vacuum. There is no heating involved at any stage. Fruits and vegetables, instant coffees are processed by freeze drying. Freeze drying produces better quality of foods, but is expensive.

Most of the foods are processed by way of dehydration. Such products are bakery products, cereal-based snack products, milk powders, juice powders, vegetables, etc. Selection of the equipment is decided on the basis of the food item, and quantity and quality of the end product desired. In India, most processed foods are manufactured by large companies and also by small-scale or tiny units. The coexistence of products manufactured in the organized and unorganized sectors is because of price differences. Manufacturers in the small scale and tiny sectors have certain advantages. They do not pay tax due to exemption limits and/or by tax evasion. They have low overhead expenses of marketing and production. They operate in rural areas where the marketing network of large companies is poor, and in the absence of competition, they are able to sell products of poor quality. It is estimated that the quantum of production of items such as bakery products, soft drinks, pickels and *chutneys*, snack foods and ice creams by small-scale or tiny units, is almost equal, or even more in some cases, than products produced in the organized sector.

The equipment for small units is of batch type, whereas in the case of large units, it is of continuous type. For large-scale production, the equipment is designed on sound principles of science and engineering, and its working is very sophisticated. It is designed taking into account production, quality issues, energy issues, cost issues, ease of operation and cleaning and sanitization issues. In the small scale and tiny units, such issues are not addressed, since there is little awareness of such issues, and/or they simply cannot afford to invest in sophisticated equipment.

## Sterilization / Aseptic Packaging

The principle of sterilization is mainly used in the canning industry, and in the case of products sold in tetrapaks. The principle of sterilization (free of living micro-organisms) for food preservation was first applied by a Frenchman Nicholas Appert in 1809. Napoleon had offered a prize of 12,000 francs for developing a process to preserve food for his army. Initially, food in glass bottles was sterilized, but by the 1860s canning in tin cans became popular. In the process of canning, food in brine, or a sugar solution, or in liquid form, is placed in a can, made out of tinplate or aluminum. The contents of the can are heated, so that the hot air escapes from the can. After heating, the can is sealed with an airtight lid, when the food is hot inside. The process of sealing creates a partial vacuum in the can. Immediately after packing, the cans are sterilized in an autoclave, at a temperature higher than 105°C for a sufficient time, so as to make the product sterile. The canned product can then be stored for a long period. In case the can develops even a minute leakage, the can bulges due to microbiological contamination, causing gas formation inside the can. Obviously, such contaminated food should not be consumed.

The process of canning is widely used for preserving mango pulp, tomato puree, sliced or cut fruits and vegetables, *rasgullas*, etc. Once a container is opened, the product does not remain sterile, and therefore it must be consumed immediately.

In 1951, the concept of sterilization was modified and applied for packing and preservation of milk, juices, fruits drinks, vegetable products, etc., by a company known as *Tetra Pak,* a multinational of Swedish origin. The company developed a special packing material made of polyethylene film, aluminum foil and paper, for making fully airtight cartons in tetrahedral shape leading to the company's name. The packing material has six layers made of 73 per cent paper board, 22 per cent plastic and 5 per cent aluminum. The company also developed an aseptic filler to fill a liquid product treated at ultra high temperatures (UHT) to fill these cartons. The system of aseptic filler and packing material allows perishable goods to be preserved and distributed over greater distances, without the need for a cold chain. Perishable products such as milk can be stored up to one year. The product offers cost advantages in terms of transport, storage, etc. The company till recently enjoyed a monopoly all over the world, and their revenue in 2010 was £9.98 billion. Recently an alternative supplier, called *Great View Aseptic Packing* headquartered in Beijing, has come up with an annual capacity of 18 billion packs.

## Refrigeration

Long ago, people observed that foods remained fresh at low temperatures. This is because at low temperatures, metabolic activities cannot take place and microbes cannot grow or multiply. Most microbes require a temperature of around 37°C to survive and grow (almost the same as in the case of human beings). There are, however, some microbes capable of growing at low temperatures and therefore, foods need to be stored at sub zero temperatures. Many foods in a raw condition are highly perishable, and they are not only stored in frozen conditions, but should be maintained in that state till consumed. Meat, fruits and vegetables and marine products are typical examples. There is always a danger of rising temperatures, i.e. breaking of the cold chain, due to electricity failures and damage to the insulating material during transportation. In general, mechanically maintained refrigeration is an expensive proposition, but is used very widely due to marketing requirements.

There are huge-sized cold storages throughout the country for storing farm produce. At processing sites also, walk-in type cold storages are available. At the point of sale, there are a variety of refrigeration equipment in which products are displayed. For transportation, insulated vans are used, and for short distances, ice or dry ice is used. Dry Ice is a solid form of carbon dioxide. It does not contain water.

No matter which process or machinery and equipment are used, in the handling of foods, there is always a need for Good Manufacturing Practices (GMP) and proper sanitation to prevent serious problems of public health hazards.

Testing of products in the laboratory is not always adequate to prevent a problem, since testing is done to check only certain parameters. Contamination of products with microbes or hazardous chemicals, even in micro quantities, is capable of creating serious problems, which may go unnoticed in routine quality control check-ups. Such instances of outbreaks of contamination keep on happening in most parts of the world.

In GMP codes, general guidelines are specified for buildings, machinery and equipment, and also employees. In the case of buildings, specifications are given regarding materials to be used, space required, design criteria, etc. The processing area must be insect proof, well-lit and ventilated, flooring should be easily washable, and there should be proper drainage facilities. Storage areas should be separated from the processing areas. Materials should be stored away from walls, on wooden or metal planks, such that there is enough air circulation. Machinery and equipment is to be so designed, that contact parts do not react with the food, and it should be easy to clean the equipment. Normally tanks, pumps, pipes, etc., are made of stainless steel and have mirror polish so that product does not stick on the surfaces. Similarly, all welding joints and curves are very smooth. The design should be such that when the equipment is washed, the water is self-draining, and there is no accumulation. After use, the equipment is first cleaned and then sanitized with disinfectants like chlorine compound, or ozone compound, or hot water or steam. Before they are used again, they are nearly sterile, free of any residue of cleaning, or disinfecting agents and odour.

In the case of employees, management has to make sure that no employee is a carrier of any contagious disease. Employees must follow a strict discipline of washing hands and drying them with hot air, before they get to work. They must put on an apron, hand gloves, cap, etc. They need to be trained for maintaining cleanliness and proper hygienic and sanitary conditions.

In addition to the general guidelines, a manufacturer has to study his own working and develop and improve the GMP at his end. These days, one cannot rule out the possibility of mischief by a careless employee, or employees who want to settle grievances with the management. Only a good GMP can prevent a mishap.

## EMERGING PROCESSING TECHNOLOGIES

Preservation technologies discussed earlier, affect the sensory (taste, smell, appearance) and nutritional properties of foods. In order to overcome these problems, new technologies are being constantly explored. Promising amongst them are:

- Irradiation
- Ultrasound
- Ultraviolet
- High hydrostatic pressure
- High voltage arc discharge
- Pulse electric field

All of these technologies are non-thermal and are effective against reducing microbial load, and in eliminating pathogenic microorganisms, and they help in increasing the shelf life of certain products. Radiation preservation is regulated by the Atomic Energy (Control of Irradiation of Foods), 1996 Rules and FSSA Rules. The following table gives details of food items approved for irradiation treatment.

**Table 3.1:** Food Items Approved for Irradiation under the Food Safety and Standard Rules 2006

| *Food Item* | *Purpose* | *Min. Dose (KGy)*** | *Max. Dose (KGy)*** |
|---|---|---|---|
| Onions | Sprout Inhibition | 0.03 | 0.09 |
| Potatoes | Sprout Inhibition | 0.06 | 0.15 |
| Ginger, Garlic, Shallots | Sprout Inhibition | 0.03 | 0.15 |
| Mango | Disinfestation | 0.25 | 0.75 |
| Raisins, Figs, Dried Dates | Disinfestation | 0.25 | 0.75 |
| Semolina, Rice, Wheat Atta and Maida | Disinfestation | 0.25 | 1.0 |
| Meat and Meat Products including Chicken | Shelf Life extension and Pathogen Control | 2.5 | 4.0 |
| Sea Foods – Fresh | Shelf Life Control | 1.0 | 3.0 |
| Sea Foods – Frozen | Pathogen Control | 4.0 | 6.0 |
| Sea Foods – Dried | Disinfestation | 0.25 | 1.0 |
| Pulses | Disinfestation | 0.25 | 1.0 |
| Spices | Microbial Decontamination | 6.0 | 14.0 |

** KGy (Kilo Gray): One kilo gray is 1000 joule of energy absorbed per kilogram of irradiated product.

## PROBLEMS ENCOUNTERED DURING AND AFTER PROCESSING

Foods are very complex in nature, made up of a variety of proteins, carbohydrates, fats, fibres, minerals, vitamins, etc. These biochemicals undergo chemical reactions during processing and storage. There are many chemical reactions that happen due to oxygen, or are oxidative in nature. Chemical reactions bring about a lot of changes in foods in terms of appearance, taste and texture. Many fruits and vegetables change colour when cut, and are exposed to air. When potato chips are fried, they turn brown during frying, due to reducing sugars present in the potatoes. Potato chips become rancid during storage, due to the fat undergoing oxidative chemical changes. When milk is acidified, by addition of acid, or due to bacterial growth, it breaks down into water and results in the precipitation of protein. The same milk cannot be brought back to its original emulsion state. In many foods, proteins undergo changes, and they are denatured, i.e. their structure and function gets changed, and they cause several problems. Interaction between proteins, carbohydrates and fibres cause problems of a rheological nature. As a result, products sometimes become gummy, sticky, rigid and hard. In the manufacture of *chikki,* concentrated sugar syrup is made by boiling sugar in water, and then nuts and other materials such as sesame seeds are mixed by stirring, and the mixture mass is quickly poured onto trays and rolled into sheets of the desired thickness. These sheets are cut into pieces and then on standing, the product solidifies and is ready to be eaten. A company tried to make *chikki* on a machine, so as to have a continuous process. It failed, because the hot mass did not remain in a fluid and pliable state, and became rock solid before the process finished. The pliability of the mass was for a short period at a critical point.

In a beer manufacturing company, the master brewer resigned due to differences with the management, and he was allowed to go, assuming his assistant would be able to handle the production. Interestingly, the beer produced by the assistant could not be bottled due to serious foaming problems, i.e. bubble formation at the top of the liquid surface resulting in liquid coming out of the container.

After lots of trials and financial losses, the company had to invite the master brewer back. The foaming problem was caused due to very minute changes in the fermentation process, which only the master brewer was aware of. In a similar case of foaming, in a soft drinks bottling plant, it was traced to the colour which was less than 0.3 per cent by weight of the total product. The problem was corrected by making minute changes in the manufacturing process of the colour.

Many problems arise during storage of products. Dehydrated products, which are free flowing, have a strong affinity for moisture, and if the products are not packed properly, they will absorb moisture from the atmosphere. The absorption of moisture causes problems of caking in the foods, affecting solubility, taste, etc. Sometimes, microbial growth takes place, and products are rendered unfit for consumption. Of course, microbiological contamination can be noticed as mold growth, which can be seen with the naked eyes. In case of growth of yeast, products get fermented and produce gas. In case of bacteria, aroma and taste of the product changes drastically. They are capable of producing toxins, which, if consumed, could be fatal. Cereals and cocoa-based products produce weevils after absorbing moisture. Thousands of tonnes of cereals rot every year, due to improper storage of cereals by the Food Corporation of India (FCI), a government agency. Cereals can be properly stored in specially designed silos.

Food companies of repute carry out shelf life studies of new products, before introducing them in the market. There are however quality issues which arise once in a while, but they are caused due to product abuse in the market.

Product abuse takes place during transportation, storage and at the retailers end. One of the most common problems is faced by marketers of frozen foods, such as ice cream, meat, etc. It is important that the cold chain is maintained from the factory to the consumer, but due to breakdowns, non-availability of power at the retailers end, accidents on road, etc., quality of the product gets affected. Most products sold under refrigeration are perishable, and they have a huge population of microbes. If temperature rises during transportation, or at the retail outlet, the microbial count increases and crosses permissible limits. The problem of high microbial count in many primary foods such as milk, meat, etc., is due to their improper handling by producers. In case of other products also, very little attention is paid to the hygienic conditions of the vehicle. At times, articles of food get contaminated with dangerous chemicals, if the trucks are not cleaned and washed properly. In open body trucks, products get exposed to sunlight and rain. Due to jerks, especially on rough roads lids of the containers get loosened, and the containers start leaking. Recently, the author came across an interesting incident of product abuse, where the company suffered huge financial losses. The company packed aluminum cans of carbonated drinks in very sturdy cartons. Due to shortage of space in the godowns, these cartons were stacked in such a way that they were used for formation of steps on which labourers climbed up carrying heavy goods. This caused leakages in the cans packed in cartons. Also, many times the cartons are stacked very high due to shortage of space, thus damaging the packs that are at the bottom of the stack. High humidity during transportation, and storage causes caking in powder products, and occasional problems of weevils in some products.

During storage, problems are caused by high temperatures and storage of other materials, particularly having a strong odour. The godowns of transporters have tin roofs and in the summer season, the temperatures inside the godown can get as high as 50°C. At such high temperatures, the shelf life of many products is shortened. There is a serious problem of rodents in transporters godowns, which damages packages of the product.

At the retailer's level, apart from the rodent problem, sometimes problems are caused due to direct exposure of the product packed in glass bottles or PET bottles to direct sunlight. Many retailers stack products outside their shops in India, thus exposing them to direct sunlight. Sunlight is capable of causing lots of changes in the basic composition of the product. It is known to discolour the product, and oxidize Vitamin C and other nutrients.

Companies of repute carry out shelf life studies in the laboratory, where accelerated shelf life studies can be carried out by exposing the product to high temperatures and humidity conditions in special equipment, where such conditions can be created and controlled. Based on such accelerated studies, they then decide about the expiry date. Of course, most products do change, compared to fresh products, but the decision on shelf life is taken on the basis of the level of acceptance, in terms of taste and appearance. In case of products making nutrition claims, they must comply with the declared nutritional values till the declared expiry date. In such cases, manufacturers take care of losses of nutrients by adding overages, i.e. addition of extra quantities of nutrients. In most cases, the product after expiry date, does not become injurious to health, but does not deliver the promised benefits, and is not acceptable in terms of taste, smell, appearance, etc. It is for this reason that many foods declare their shelf life as *Best Before When Used By* and not as an *Expiry Date*. In the case of medicines, the expiry date has a different purpose. It assures the efficacy of the medicine, if used before the expiry date.

There is always a conflict about the shelf life, between the technical and marketing people of a company. Technical people try to indicate a shorter life to ensure that the product stays as perfect as possible till such time that the consumer consumes it. On the other hand, marketing people demand a longer shelf life, since it gives them additional time for the product to remain on the shelf and be sold. In case of new products, the marketing people are not confident about the demand in the marketplace. Hence, they want a longer period to sell the product. In case if the product remains unsold on the shelf after the expiry date, the product needs to be taken back. In such cases they have to offer special schemes to the consumers to liquidate the stock. The issue of shelf life does not arise in the case of well established brands of food products. In the developed countries, food products are consumed within three to four weeks from the date of manufacture. In India the minimum time required is six months for certain products, and in the case of new products, almost 12 months.

Once in a while, products are deliberately abused by mischievous customers to blackmail manufacturers. They do so by tampering with the packing, and putting foreign matter like insects, flies, etc., into the product. Of course, at times, there are some genuine quality problems also created either due to men, materials or machines, involved in the manufacture of the products.

Another important issue is of water and waste disposal. The role of water in the food industry is very crucial. Some of the liquid products such as soft drinks, and ready to drink beverages contain almost 87 per cent water. Many other products also contain water to some extent. In other words, water is a critical raw material for the food industry. For this reason, its quality and availability is an important issue. A number of food companies did not pay any attention to this issue when they selected the site of their factory. For selection of the site, other commercial factors were considered, but the role of water was taken for granted. They did not realize that water treatment could be an expensive proposition on a perpetual basis, to maintain the quality of the product, preventing scaling in the machinery and equipment, etc. Many a time, production is affected in spite of demand in the market, due to non-availability of water. Most of the food products are sold on the basis of impulse buying, and therefore non-availability causes loss of sale. At present, 90 per cent of the water is used in agriculture, about 7 per cent is used by people for drinking and other purposes and about 2 per cent by industries. There is already scarcity of water in the big cities and towns, and this will increase once the demand for water by industry also grows. Selling water has become big business, and civic bodies have already started charging for supplying of water, that does not necessarily meet drinking water standards.

Sources of water are lakes, rivers and the underground. The quality of water depends on the source of the water. Lake water is relatively pure, since it is rain water. In the case of river water, due to passage of water over long distances, it contains a lot of dissolved minerals and organic matter. So is the case with underground water. Quality problems with water are of two types, namely due to chemical composition and microbial contamination. Water treatment is designed to meet the quality required for end use. For water to be used in food products, it has to be treated to reduce excessive chemicals, both inorganic and organic, and also for making it safe for consumption. Sometimes, water is found to be contaminated by pathogenic, i.e. disease causing bacteria. Their presence is detected by the presence of *coliform* bacteria, present in human and animal excreta who might be carriers of diseases. Depending on the chemical composition, water is made potable by treatment with flocculants, such as alum and ferrous sulphate, along with disinfectants like chlorine, and the water is then filtered and passed through an activated carbon bed to remove colour, odour, etc., and make it free of chlorine. Removal of chlorine is a must, since chlorine is carcinogenic, i.e. causes cancer. Many civic bodies use chlorine, but do not remove it properly.

Water needs to be made soft (removal of hardness) for prevention of scale formation during heating in boilers and in other equipment. For this purpose, water softening plants which contain ion exchange resins are used. In cases where water contains high quantity of minerals, RO (reverse osmosis) plants are used, in which the dissolved minerals are filtered out through special membranes. This process is expensive and has the disadvantage of generating almost 50 per cent water that has a high content of minerals and cannot be used for any purpose. Normally, RO plants, on a commercial scale are recommended when no drinking water is available, and sea water is to be converted for drinking purposes. Lately, RO plants combined with UV rays treatment for disinfection are being marketed for domestic use. They are sold mainly because people doubt the quality of water supplied by the authorities.

Water is also used in huge quantities for cleaning, washing, heating, cooling, etc. If water is *hard* it causes scaling in the machinery and equipment, leading to high energy costs for heat transfer. The consumption of water depends on the article of food that is being processed, but it can be almost 10 times of the quantity of the product being produced.

Another important issue is of waste disposal. Food industries generate a lot of effluents containing parts of the product, washings containing chemical compounds, etc. The effluents are food for micro-organisms, since they have a food value. It is measured in the laboratory in terms of Biochemical Oxygen Demand (BOD). Domestic sewage has a BOD of about 200 to 300 ppm, whereas effluents from the food industry BOD varies from 300 to 30000 ppm (in case of distillery waste). After 1974, there is a Water Pollution Prevention Act in force, which has laid down criteria for effluents before being discharged into the sewers, rivers, etc. For treating effluents there are methods, and treatment plants are available such as trickling filter plant, and activated sludge plant. At times, the effluents are first discharged into an oxidation lagoon in the factory, where algae grows and the BOD is lowered. Effluent treatment plants are expensive and they require a lot of space.

In the marketplace, there is a serious problem of solid waste being created by the packing materials, after consumption of the food items. The problem is not only of collection and sorting, but the difficulty in destroying them. Some plastic materials, when incinerated, produce toxic fumes. Recently, the Supreme Court has put a ban on use of plastic films by *Gutka* manufacturers. So far, the problem of solid waste disposal has not assumed very serious proportions as in the developed countries, but it is a matter of time before it becomes a serious problem in our country as well.

In conclusion, the problems of availability of water, effluent disposal and handling of solid waste have started becoming serious and it could be much worse in the future. When mega food parks, are built the agencies involved in providing infrastructure need to pay adequate attention to these problems.

# 4

# Food Additives in Processed Foods

In the processing of foods, a number of food additives are required, so as to impart characteristics like flavour, colour, texture, etc. Food additives are also used for other functions like controlling acidity, preventing moisture pick up, sweetening and prevention of spoilage due to oxidation. Under Food Safety and Standards Authority of India (FSSA) Rules, about five hundred and fifty-five additives are permitted in India at present, whereas the latest edition of the *Food Chemicals Codex* published by the US Food and Drug Administration (FDA) covers details of about eleven hundred such additives. Use of food additives is increasing in food processing, but experts the world over are concerned about the safety of the foods consumed by people. Since the trade in processed foods is increasing between countries, the need was felt for uniform specifications and regulations. It is for this reason, an International Numbering System (INS) is followed. Each food additive is given a unique INS number, and processed food manufacturers are required to indicate the INS number, or the name of the additive when giving details of the ingredients on a food package. Annexure A provides a detailed list of additives sorted by INS number. In the case of flavouring agents, giving the INS number is not feasible, since it is not made of a single chemical/material, and are of different types. In view of this, a food processor is required to separately give a statement

*CONTAINS ADDED FLAVOUR* giving details of the nature and common name of the flavour. In the following paragraphs, various functions performed by food additives in processed foods are explained.

## FLAVOURING AGENTS

The definition of flavouring agents under FSSA rules is as follows:

*Flavouring agents include flavour substances, flavour extracts or flavour preparations which are capable of imparting flavouring properties, namely taste or odour or both to food.*

Flavouring agents can be of the following three types as defined under FSSA rules:

(a) **Natural Flavours and Natural Flavouring Substances.** Natural flavours and natural flavouring substances are flavour preparations and single substances respectively, acceptable for human consumption, obtained exclusively by a physical process from vegetables for human consumption.

(b) **Nature Identical Flavouring Substances.** Nature identical flavouring substances, are substances chemically isolated from aromatic raw materials, or obtained synthetically. They are chemically identical to substances present in natural products, intended for human consumption, either processed or not.

(c) **Artificial Flavouring Substances.** Artificial flavouring substances are those substances which have not been identified in natural products, intended for human consumption, either processed or not.

To understand the differences of these flavour categories, one can take the example of the Vanilla flavour.

When a vanilla extract is prepared, using natural vanilla beans and solvent, it is an example of a natural flavour.

In the same extract, when a substance vanillin is added, the flavour has to be declared per (b) i.e. nature identical, and when a substance ethyl vanillin is mixed, the resultant flavour will have to be declared as per (c) or artificial. In case of (b), vanillin is found in a natural product, i.e. in vanilla extract, but the added vanillin has been produced externally in a factory by a chemical reaction. In case of ethyl vanillin, it is not only produced externally by a chemical reaction, but its presence has not been confirmed in natural vanilla beans.

All food products have their own taste properties. Less than 0.2 per cent of the chemicals present in food are responsible for the taste of the product. A flavour chemist has intimate knowledge of the chemicals that are responsible for the taste. For example, the peel of orange fruit is rich in the typical aroma of orange fruits. It is possible to extract, or isolate the portion which is rich in aroma by way of distillation, or by another process. This material is known as orange oil, which is called an essential oil. It is subjected to analysis in the laboratory, and found to contain several aromatic chemicals. This knowledge helps the chemist in duplicating the orange aroma and taste, by compounding such aromatic chemicals synthetically produced in the correct proportion, and diluting it to the level present in a natural orange, thereby giving the taste and aroma of orange flavour. There are hundreds of aromatic chemicals which have been identified in several natural products, and flavour chemists are successful in duplicating their taste. Health authorities publish lists of chemicals from time to time, declaring them as Generally Recognized As Safe (GRAS) for use in flavours.

Many people feel that synthetic flavours are harmful and natural flavours are safe. This is not always so. They are not aware of the fact, that even in synthetic flavours, a majority of the aromatic chemicals present are present in nature, and there are only some chemicals whose presence is not confirmed in nature. All these chemicals have been tested extensively by the health authorities, to see if they are harmful for consumption. For their use in flavours, specifications are provided by experts, and only those aromatic chemicals meeting flavour grade specifications are permitted to be used by flavour manufacturers.

On the other hand, it is assumed that all natural products are safe, but again, this is a generalization. A number of natural products, including some spices, which we consume on a daily basis, are found to contain toxic materials which have been found to be carcinogenic in animal trials. Of course many natural products and spices contain antioxidants, which are found to contain anti-carcinogenic and anti-ageing properties. Considering these facts, it is safe to say that nature identical flavours are the best to be used, since they are safer, although they may not have any beneficial properties.

The selection of the flavour type whether natural, nature identical, or artificial, that is to be used in any food product, is dependent on multiple factors. Amongst them are taste, desired shelf life, cost, consistency and availability. Nature identical and artificial flavours offer advantages in terms of shelf life, cost, consistency and availability, whereas natural flavours offer advantages in terms of being perceived as harmless, or rather healthy.

Any food manufacturer, or formulator, must weigh all these factors carefully to decide what to use. Also, it is important to note that due to various factors described earlier, different flavours are commonly available as a specific flavour type(s) only – for example, a spice flavour like black pepper, or ginger, or cardamom, would generally be available as a natural flavour, whereas most fruit flavours like orange, lemon, pineapple, etc., are typically available as nature identical, or artificial forms. Some flavours would be available in two, or all three formats.

The flavour industry plays a pivotal role in the success or failure of the final product in the market, though many a times, the flavour is the least expensive component in the overall cost of the product. Flavours are used in bakery products, soft drinks, beverages, ice-creams, confectionery items, oral care products, hard drinks, etc.

There is good scope for the export of several flavouring raw materials, such as spice oils, oleoresins, essential oils, aromatic chemicals, etc. Also, local demand for these materials is increasing, which could benefit farmers.

## FOOD COLOURS

They are used in foods to enhance appearance, and make them more pleasing to the eye. The good appearance of a product influences the decision of the consumer to try the product, and increases the acceptability of the product. Imagine, if all the soft drinks such as cola, orange, mango pineapple, etc., were colourless. Taste, smell and colour are interlinked in the acceptability quotient of the product, just as taste and smell alone would not give as much enjoyment, as when combined with colour.

FSSA Rules have devoted a whole section covering various aspects, such as unauthorized addition of prohibited colouring matter, extraneous additions to be declared, and the maximum limit of colours to be used, etc. Detection of unauthorized synthetic colours in any food product is very easy, and the majority of food related cases in courts in India, are related to colour addition.

There are two types of colours – natural and synthetic. FSSA Rules provide a list of both types of colours. No matter which type of colours are added, a separate statement is to be made on the pack stating:

*Contains Permitted Natural Colour(s)*

For example, cola drinks contain caramel which is a natural colour produced by the burning of sugar.

Or

*Contains Permitted Synthetic Food Colour(s)*

For example, most soft drinks, hard boiled candies, ice creams, etc., contain only synthetic colours.

Or

*Contains Permitted Natural and Synthetic Food Colour(s)*

The quality of the colours should be as per BIS (Bureau of Indian Standards), and also their INS numbers need to be mentioned in the list of ingredients.

## EMULSIFYING AND STABILIZING AGENTS

This is another extremely important category of food additives. The definition given under FSSA Rules states, 'emulsifying agents and stabilizing agents means substances which, when added to food, are capable of facilitating uniform dispersion of oils and fats in aqueous media, or vice versa and/or stabilizing such emulsions.'

Imagine a glass that is half filled with water, and another filled with oil. Mix the contents of both the glasses and stir vigorously. You will observe a non-transparent mass consisting of small drops of oil, or water phase, dispersed throughout the continuous phase of the other liquid. What you observe is an emulsion, and without the aid of an emulsifier, the emulsion will eventually separate back into the original components.

Emulsifiers are substances which reduce the surface tension at the interface of two normally immiscible phases, allowing them to mix and form a homogenous emulsion. Stabilizers are a group of compounds which help in stabilizing emulsions.

The key functions of emulsifiers may be summarized as:

1. To promote emulsion stability, stabilize aerated systems, and control agglomeration of fat globules.
2. To modify texture, shelf life, and rheological properties by complexing with starch and protein components, and
3. To improve the texture of fat-based foods by controlling the polymorphism of fats.

Examples of products to which emulsifiers are added are bakery products, such as bread, cakes, ice-creams and other frozen confectioneries, pastas, processed meats, margarine and low calorie spreads, salad dressings, extruded products, etc.

Soft drinks, particularly cloudy orange and lemon flavoured drinks, are prepared by using flavours in emulsion form. If flavours are directly added, then they will skim off, and a ring will be formed at the neck of the bottle.

## ACIDIFYING AGENTS/ACIDITY REGULATORS

There are several products in which acids are added extraneously for imparting taste, and for extending the shelf life of the products. There are several natural fruit products which contain acids such as citric acid, malic acid, tartaric acid, lactic acid, acetic acid etc. Soft drinks and candies use large quantities of citric acid, which is imported into India.

In the manufacture of cola flavoured drinks, phosphoric acid is used. Phosphoric acid is an inorganic acid, and many people have doubts about its safety. There are a number of myths that appear in the media such as teeth getting dissolved in a cola drink. But all such observations though true, are misleading. The same tooth would get dissolved in any product which is acidic. Fruit juices, butter milk, etc., are also acidic. The gastric juice produced in our stomach is highly acidic, because it contains concentrated hydrochloric acid, which is also an inorganic acid.

Soft drinks and hard boiled candies are the major categories of products which contain acids.

## SWEETENERS

In place of sugar, several sweeteners are used. Basically, they are of two types:

Those that are essentially calorie free, often referred to as non-nutritive sweeteners, and those that significantly reduce calories, which are called reduced calorie sweeteners, bulk sweeteners or sugar replacers.

There is no ideal sweetener that presently exists. The ideal sweetener must be compatible with a wide range of food ingredients, because sweetness is but one element of a complex food flavour system. Since, several sweeteners are available, food manufacturers need to use sweeteners that are best suited for a particular application. For example, some sweeteners break down under heat. Therefore, such sweeteners cannot be used in any food products that involve heat treatment during manufacture. Also, limitations of individual sweeteners can be overcome by using them in blends. Most sweeteners are synergistic, which means that the sweetness of the sweetener blend is greater, than the sum of individual parts. It is important to remember, that in developing low calorie food products, low calorie sweeteners cannot easily substitute sugar. Common sugar has many other functions in the product, besides providing sweetness. Table 4.1 lists some functional properties of sugar. Table 4.2 gives details of relative sweetness of different sweeteners.

**Table 4.1:** Some Functional Properties of Sugar

| |
|---|
| Browning Reactions |
| Fermentability |
| Flavour enhancement |
| Freezing point depression |
| Nutritive solids source |
| Osmotic pressure |
| Sweetness |
| Texture tenderizer |
| Viscosity/bodying agent |

There are five low calorie (non-nutritive) sweeteners that are permitted in foods under FSSA Rules. They are saccharin, aspartame, acesulfame potassium (K), sucralose and neotame.

Saccharin was discovered by Remsen and Fahlberg at the Johns Hopkins University in the US in 1899. It is 300 to 400 times sweeter than sugar. It has a bitter, metallic and astringent after taste. But, after another sweetener cyclamate was discovered in 1934, and when the first commercial blend of saccharin and cyclamate was marketed, people discovered that saccharin boosted the sweetening power of cyclamate, while cyclamate masked the after taste of saccharin. This synergistic effect benefited soft drink manufacturers. In 1979, the use of cyclamate was banned in the US and in many other countries, though it is still permitted in about 50 countries. Though saccharin has been available for more than 100 years, in 1977 the FDA in the US proposed a ban on it, on the basis of controversial high dose rat studies, in which rats that were fed the human equivalent of sodium saccharin of hundreds of cans of diet soft drinks per day for a lifetime, showed development of tumours in the bladder. The US Congress placed a moratorium on the proposed ban, since consumers were up in arms and challenged the findings of the authorities. It was then decided, that products containing saccharin, would bear a warning on the label, indicating that saccharin had been shown to cause tumours in laboratory animals. In 1991, FDA withdrew its proposal for the ban. In 2000, the US National Toxicology Programme delisted saccharin from its list of potential carcinogens, and as a result, Congress removed the saccharin label warning requirement.

**Table 4.2:** Relative Sweetness of Sweeteners

| *Sugar* | *Index* |
|---|---|
| Sucrose (Common Sugar) | 100 |
| Dextrose (Glucose) | 70-80 |
| Levulose (Fructose) | 140 |
| 70-DE corn syrup | 70-75 |
| High conversion corn syrup | 65 |
| Regular conversion corn syrup | 50 |
| Maltose | 30-50 |
| Lactose | 20 |
| High fructose corn syrup | |
| 90 per cent | 120-160 |
| 55 per cent | >100 |
| 42 per cent | 100 |
| Invert sugar | >100 |
| Sorbitol | 50 |
| Xylitol | 100 |
| Saccharine (Non-nutritive sweetener) | >40,000 |
| Aspartame (Non-nutritive sweetener) | 18000-20000 |
| Acesulfame – K (Non-nutritive sweetener) | 20000 |
| Sucralose (Non-nutritive sweetener) | 60000 |
| Neotame (Non-nutritive sweetener) | 700000 |

Aspartame is another widely used sweetener which is almost 180 to 200 times sweeter than sugar. Aspartame is a dipeptide – a type of protein by nature, and is susceptible to breaking down on prolonged heating. Aspartame was discovered in 1965, when a pharmaceutical company was trying to synthesize a product for ulcer therapy. Its use was approved in 1981. There were a lot of questions raised by critics about its safety, but the US FDA has stated, that aspartame is one of the most thoroughly tested food additives ever submitted to the agency. Also, a French food safety agency conducted an extensive review of aspartame, promoted by negative allegations about it, and determined that there is no scientific data to support such allegations.

In 1969, Acesulfame K was discovered by Nutrinova Inc. which was approved for use in the US in 1988. It is also 200 times sweeter than sugar and generally used in combination with aspartame. Unlike aspartame, it is heat stable, and does not break down on prolonged heating.

Sucralose is 600 times sweeter than sugar, and was approved in 1998. It was introduced by Johnson and Johnson in the US. It does not have a bitter taste, and it can withstand heat. It is used in soft drinks, bakery products and confectionary items. It is also sold as a table top sweetener.

The newest entrant in the Indian market is Neotame, which is almost 7000 times sweeter than sugar. It is stable across a wide range of applications, and is similar in stability to aspartame, but has greater stability in baked and dairy products.

Since the low calorie (non-nutritive) sweeteners are many hundred times sweeter than sugar, replacing sugar in foods with such sweeteners often leads to a dramatic reduction in the bulk, or mass of the product. In such cases, there is another class of sweeteners that are combined with non-nutritive sweeteners to provide bulk and improve texture and mouth feels of the food. These sweeteners are called polyols, and they have less than four calories per gram (varying in the range of 2kcal per gram to 3 kcal per gram). There are eight polyols currently used – namely erythritol, mannitol, isomalt, lactitol, maltitol, xylitol, sorbitol and hydrogenated starch hydrolysates.

To claim reduced calories, a product must have at least 25 per cent less calories than its traditional full calorie counterpart.

Products made using a combination of non-nutritive sweeteners (like aspartame, acesulfame K) and polyols are allowed to claim being sugar-free in the United States, as per FDA rules. It is easier to use sweeteners in place of sugar in liquid products such as tea, coffee, soft drinks, etc. Replacement of sugar in other products is not so simple, since it is difficult to match the functional properties of sugar.

## ANTI-CAKING AGENTS

Many powder products particularly those which are dried by removing moisture, have an affinity for moisture, and when they are exposed to humidity, they absorb moisture from the atmosphere and cake. In food processing, a number of food products are dehydrated, and to prevent them from reabsorbing moisture from the atmosphere, they are mixed with anti-caking agents. These agents are light in weight, and when they are mixed with the product, they provide a coating on the surface that acts as a deterrent, and protects food from coming in touch with moisture in the air. Also, they make products free flowing. Table top common salt is known to cake in the rainy season, but refined salt manufacturers are permitted to use anti-caking agents such as silicates, up to 2 per cent, to keep the salt free flowing. Current FSSA Rules permit use of anti-caking agents only in salt, onion powder, garlic powder, fruit powder and soup powder. Tricalcium phosphate (TCP) is also used, which is also a nutrient and serves as a source of calcium.

## ANTI-OXIDANTS

Anti-oxidant means a substance, which when added to food retards or prevents oxidative deterioration of food. There are no restrictions for using natural anti-oxidants such as Vitamin C and E and lecithin, but synthetic additives are permitted only in edible oils and fats (except ghee and butter). Oxidative change in edible oil is identified by a rancid taste. The nutritional and health benefits of anti-oxidants are covered in detail in Chapter 9 Nutrition and Lifestyle Diseases.

## SAFETY OF FOOD ADDITIVES

Many consumers of processed foods have doubts about the harmful effects of additives. They think that additives are chemicals and therefore must be harmful. They do not imagine that the food they consume, is also a complex mixture of chemicals. To expel doubts of such people, they should be assured that permitted food additives are the least harmful substances present in food. Their use in foods is permitted by health authorities the world over after a lot of studies by experts. Safety data is collected by pharmacological studies in which studies are carried out on animals by feeding them several times more quantity than the average daily intake (ADI) of a human being. Once safety is established, it is permitted for use, but with certain conditions. Quality standards are prescribed for the additives. Also, maximum limits are prescribed for their use. Studies also ensure that the additive does not interfere with the testing of the other parameters of the quality prescribed.

Organizations like the WHO (World Health Organization) (a division of the United Nations), FDA of the US, health authorities of the European Union etc. and the Ministry of Health in India, have since the last several decades, involved several expert committees for allowing the use of additives. In the US, the Food and Nutrition Board was established as early as 1940 to study food additives. In India, in 1955, the Central Committee of Food Standards was formed. It formed a subcommittee on the subject of food additives. On this subcommittee, representation was given to industry and the author had the pleasure of representing his employer on the committee to examine the needs for allowing particular additives, or banning particular additives, if they were found harmful. Under the present FSSA Act, there is a Central Advisory Committee under which several scientific panels will work as subcommittees. One of them is on the subject of food additives.

Use of food additives in the processed food industry is inevitable, for several reasons and authorities are strict regarding their safety and use. Most additives are permitted at the level of parts per million (ppm). One ppm is one gram in 1000 kgs, i.e. one tonne. If you consider the quantity of staples and regular food and processed packed foods that you are consuming everyday, and work out your total intake of food additives, you will find they are in miniscule quantities and that too of high quality of tried and tested material. It is worth mentioning, that most additives have a long history of consumption, without any health problems being attributed to them.

In India the safety aspect is more important in case of primary foods, due to excessive use of chemicals, improper storage, etc., rather than issues related to food additives.

# 5

# Quality Control of Processed Foods

In the case of most manufactured goods, quality evaluation is done by physical, chemical or biological (in the case of pharmaceuticals) methods. Physical objects can be weighed, measured and tested by the prescribed methods of testing. For almost all such products, there are some reliable and objective methods of testing and proper measuring instruments to carry out such testing. In case of foods such objective testing may not always be possible, since taste and smell are very subjective in nature. There is no known instrument right now that can give an objective, or quantifiable measure of taste, or smell. Therefore, testing is mainly sensory, or organoleptic – which means that the food is evaluated by a panel of experts using their senses through their nose, tongue and eyes, and the product is compared with an approved reference. In addition, basic chemical and microbiological analysis is carried out on raw materials and finished goods, which ensure safety and compliance with food regulations.

Not many people, including some manufacturers, are aware that quality control activities can help in improving production efficiency, and controlling costs, thus saving money. To support this view, two examples are described as follows:

In the nineteenth century, guns were handmade, and all parts were made separately and assembled by making changes in the parts, so that they properly fit in their places to make a gun. A gentleman named Whitney, took a contract to supply a huge quantity of guns to the federal government of the US. When an inspector from the federal government came to visit his factory, Mr. Whitney was not able to show even a single piece, since none was ready. It was assumed that no supply would be made by the committed date. But on the date of delivery, the inspector was amazed to see a huge pile of guns. Mr. Whitney had standardized all the parts, and they were made within very precise parameters. As a result, his men could assemble guns just by picking up parts at random, without choosing, thus resulting in very high speeds of production.

In case of cost savings the following is a true experience. In soft drinks manufacturing, glass bottles are used, and they are collected back from the market and then washed for use again. This way, the glass bottle is used several times, before it is destroyed. A soft drink manufacturer placed an order with a new supplier, and received bottles looking almost the same, and having the same height as what he was using. In automatic bottling plants, the contents of the bottles are regulated by a fill height, which is measured from the top of the bottle. In the supplies that he received, the contents of the bottle were higher by 5 per cent for the same fill height, compared to his regular bottles. Once the bottles of this supply got mixed with his regular bottles, it was impossible to distinguish between the two. In other words, every time the bottles were filled, a 5 per cent extra quantity of the finished soft drink would go into the market. Taking into account the cost of the liquid material, and also the number of times the bottles were likely to be filled, it was cheaper to destroy the bottles.

Also, it is always a very costly, unpleasant and an extremely difficult job to recall a product from the market, on account of quality issues. There is also a very high intangible cost due to loss of reputation in the market.

It is beyond the scope of this book to go into technical details of chemical and microbiological analysis of foods, but some issues are highlighted, that arise due to discrepancies in analytical results. Sometimes, analytical results can vary widely, when tested by different laboratories, and this can have bad consequences, especially for food products. For example, until recently, under PFA rules, if a sample was found not conforming to the standards laid down, the sample was declared *adulterated,* instead of *sub-standard*. Note that sub-standard is when a parameter is not as per the prescribed limits. This may happen due to mistakes in manufacturing, or differences in analytical results. Adulteration is a deliberate action by the manufacturer to deliver a bad quality product, with the intention to reduce costs. The charge of adulteration is a cognizable offence, and attracts a minimum punishment of six months rigorous imprisonment. Present FSSA regulations have now been rectified, where a sub-standard offence attracts only economic penalties. Sometime back, during a discussion on a TV news channel about rotting of grains, a participant pointed out that several thousand tonnes of rice was rotting for two years, on account of discrepancies with respect to two parameters, namely percentage of broken and damaged pieces and moisture content. The stock under question was found to contain 6 per cent of broken and damaged pieces against the norm of 5 per cent and 14.2 per cent moisture against the norm of 14 per cent. Certainly, the stock lying in godowns could be consumed, as it is, or by mixing it with better quality rice. By allowing it to rot, it was rendered unfit for consumption.

In the case of microbiological analysis, an estimate of the population of microbes, such as bacteria, yeast and mould is made. Microbes are living organisms which cannot be seen by the naked eye, even though they are present in foods. It is possible to determine their approximate numbers in a product. A sample of the product is placed on a sterile nutrient medium in a round Petri dish. The plated sample is incubated for a certain number of hours, at a particular temperature. This results in their growth due to reproduction from one single organism to millions of organisms at the same spot, leading to the formation of a colony of the same organism, which then becomes visible to the naked eye. Presence of one colony represents one count in the original sample.

All microbes are not harmful. Our intestines are full of microbes, and they help us in digestion, and in absorption of nutrients. Because of this, there are products enriched with fibres that are sold in the market. Fibre is considered to be a prebiotic, i.e. supporting growth of good microbes in the intestine. There are wide variations in microbial counts from food to food. Raw fish contains as many as five lakh microbes per gram, whereas in an ice cream, it is up to 250,000 per gram. There are certain disease producing microbes, known as pathogenic organisms, and their presence is objectionable. FSSA Rules provide details of the limits of permissible microbes in different foods.

As mentioned earlier, the most important aspect of quality control of processed foods is sensory evaluation. After all, the proof of the pudding is in its eating.  In sensory evaluation, appearance, taste and odour are evaluated against a benchmarked approved product.

At present, we cannot adequately express, define, or explain our taste and smell sensations. Flavour is defined as a complex sensation comprising taste, odour, roughness or smoothness, hotness or coldness, and pungency or blandness. Of these qualities, odour and taste are the main contributors to flavour. We all know how flavourless foods become, when we suffer from common cold. Odour, therefore greatly affects flavour. Most people describe their opinion in simple terms like *sweet, salty, sour* and *bitter.* These are basic tastes, but food products are not just made of permutations and combinations of these four tastes. The varieties of taste and odour are so wide, that no description in words, would be adequate or perfect.

We have all experienced that with natural products, like fruits, their taste varies, even though they are from the same tree, and plucked at the same time. We accept them without complaining to anyone. Unfortunately this is not so, in the case of branded processed foods. Once a consumer likes a product, he forms a habit, and wants it to remain consistent. He is able to detect even the minutest of changes, and would complain about the changes. In case of a new flavour, he may like or may not like it, but will not complain about the quality. In view of this, maintaining uniform quality in foods is a much more challenging job, than in the case of chemicals, or even pharmaceuticals. It is a well recognized fact, that the human nose and tongue are more sensitive and powerful than manmade laboratory instruments. This is true in the case of dogs as well. It is because of their superiority in smelling and detecting chemicals, that they are trained for sniffing, and are used in criminal investigations. There are now instruments such as Gas Liquid Chromatograph (GLC), High Pressure GLC and electronic nose, etc., but they are not as powerful as our senses. Hence, many leading food companies believe in the ultimate test of quality, i.e. proof of the pudding is in the eating. They have a panel of expert tasters to evaluate quality, and decide about approval or rejection of the product.

The formation of the panel is based on their capability to distinguish between flavours. Their thresholds of taste perception is checked with materials such as quinine (bitter), hydrochloric acid (sour), sodium chloride (salty) and sucrose (sweet). They are trained by using prescribed procedures depending on the final product. They are required to smell before tasting. Tasters are required to know about nibbling and mouth-rinsing. They are explained the procedures for chewing, slurping and sucking. The most important requirement for effective sensing, is complete concentration, without distractions, while tasting the sample. There are special testing booths where samples are served from the serving place, through sliding doors. The booths are soundproof and free from any outside odours. There are special light arrangements to avoid influence of appearance, in some cases. There are many other precautions to be taken by the taster, such as washing of hands, distance to be maintained from nose while smelling, no smoking for a certain amount of time before testing the sample, etc. If the opinion of the panel is divided, then further testing is done with a larger panel, and in some cases, the opinion of a recognized professional is solicited. The author has witnessed the ability of individuals to detect smell in the final product, when most people did not notice it.

In one case, a taster was a lady whose job was to cook a TV dinner of turkey slices with the gravy, to taste. One day, she reported the presence of paint in the product. Others in the quality control laboratory did not notice this, even after it was pointed out. But, another expert, from production was invited, and he too could identify a paint smell without being told about it. There was no painting job going on in the factory, but still an investigation was carried out. It came to notice that during the night hours, when the conveyor was giving trouble, its supporting legs had to be raised by about six inches. The unpainted legs were visible, and a minor painting job was carried out for a few minutes, while continuing production. The product had absorbed the paint smell from the atmosphere. Many times, such problems arise when materials are packed in painted bulk containers.

In another case, in a flavoured soft drink concentrate, the smell of halogen was reported. After detailed investigations it was revealed that in one of the liquid ingredients there was odour of chlorine. Further investigations revealed that it came from chlorinated water supplied by the municipal corporation to the manufacturer of the ingredient.

These days, there are professional tasters working in the tea, coffee, wine and other hard drinks industries. Of course, it is not just their ability to differentiate between tastes, but also thorough training in sensory evaluation that helps.

In the early sixties, an analytical instrument called the Gas Liquid Chromatograph was introduced in the market. It deals with aromatic chemicals. It separates them from a mixture, and helps in their identification. People at that time thought that with this technique, we would know everything about the chemicals that are responsible for flavour. But to their dismay, chemists kept on finding out a large number of chemicals in food products. In other words, more and more problems of flavour kept on being discovered. It was realized that this kind of an objective method, cannot replace sensory evaluation. However, if the data collected by this method can be correlated to sensory analysis, then the objective method can be used for tests, without the unavoidable variations found by a human panel.

At times, in the manufacturing of processed foods, some changes are unavoidable, due to factors beyond control – for example, the source of supply of ingredients. In such a situation, one needs to be sure about the consistent quality of supply. It is important to find out, if a change in supply has resulted in a change that is significant enough to be noticed by the customers. In such cases, a simple triangulation test is carried out, in which two identical samples, and one different sample is given to a large panel of trained testers. Depending on the correct answers, and applying probability rules, one can find out if the change will be noticeable, or not.

As mentioned earlier, many products undergo noticeable changes in taste and appearance, but not necessarily a change in measurable parameters of quality, such as acid content, colour content, sugar content, etc.

# 6

# Packaging of Processed Foods

All processed foods must be packed in such a manner that the product remains consumable, and does not deteriorate, till it reaches the consumer. In addition, the food processor also has to consider several other issues, before selecting a proper packaging type for his food product. Some of them are:

1. Cost of the packaging material
2. Ease of packaging
3. Convenience of usage from the consumer's point of view
4. Sales appeal when the pack is displayed on the shelf
5. Pack size, or net contents of the pack
6. Cost of transportation
7. Disposal of packing material after consumption of product

In view of the above, packaging is as important an aspect, as the food product itself. Many companies that have several products, and handle large volumes, have a separate department that employs experts on packaging. They are constantly in touch with the manufacturers of packing materials, and packaging machinery and equipment.

There are many types of packing materials used for packing of processed foods. Containers made out of tinplate, aluminum and glass are used, especially where heating is involved. Aluminum and glass bottles are also used in packing of carbonated drinks. The advantage of glass is, that it does not react with the contents. Glass bottles can be repeatedly used after cleaning. They are also environment friendly. Carbonated drink manufacturers the world over, have conventionally used and are still using glass bottles. The use of PET bottles is relatively recent. However, glass containers have a disadvantage in terms of weight, space, breakage and difficulties in terms of transportation. But, repeated use makes them economical. In the case of metal cans, they can be transported and stored in flat conditions, and at the place of use they can be formed by use of a simple machine. They of course cannot be reused as is the case with glass bottles.

HDPE (High Density Polyethylene), PET (Polyethylene) and PP (Poly Propylene) are used in making rigid plastic containers. They are used in the packing of several products. These containers have proper closures, and hence, when the entire contents are not to be used at a time, the remaining product can be protected (especially from moisture) by using of closure or the lid. They are cheap, and can be easily made in different shapes and sizes. In addition, PET bottles are available as preforms that are easy to transport, and can be blown up into the final shape during use. The disadvantage of plastic containers is that they do not offer as much protection against moisture as aluminum, or glass, and the shelf life of products, especially of liquid products, is lower in plastic containers, as compared to glass or aluminum.

The technology of making flexible plastic films has revolutionized the packaging industry. These films offer many advantages. They are light in weight, can be printed, they are heat sealable, are moisture proof, they can be co-extruded with other materials, occupy much less space as they are available in rolls, and there are packing machines which use such laminates in roll forms to pack products in sachets, or bigger packs. Such machines called FFS (Form Fill Seal), offer a lot of features in terms of different shapes and sizes that they can handle, printing of statutory information such as batch number, price, etc. FFS machines are designed to handle 40-350 pouches per minute.

A consumer of processed food has very little idea about the technology that is used in packing the product. Different processed foods have different physical properties and they require special care in handling while packing. For example, carbonated drinks contain gas at high pressures and have a tendency of foaming, and are required to be filled in bottles. The foaming makes this very difficult and nearly impossible to do, but the problem was addressed by developing a high pressure filler which builds a counter pressure with air in the empty bottle, before drawing the beverage into it. In this way, the beverage flows in the bottle slowly by gravity only. The filler valve is so designed that when the correct fill height is achieved, the liquid stops flowing. The bottle is then immediately sealed. In a modern bottling plant, 1200 glass bottles per minute, i.e. 20 bottles per second are packed with accurate quantities, and without loss of gas from the product. In order to pack so many bottles, the filler also needs to be provided with empty clean bottles at that speed, and for that purpose, automatic bottle washers have been designed. To clean bottles perfectly, the washer has different stages of cleaning, such as pre-rinsing, soaking in hot caustic solution, rinsing or washing away of caustic residue, and the final rinsing with disinfected water. Bottles washed in such machines are nearly sterile. Also a beverage making system has been developed to provide beverage continuously to the filler. The entire bottling is done in hygienic conditions, and with almost hundred per cent efficiency in countries like Japan.

Another example of packing of potato chips should also be of interest. Automatic potato chip producing plants produce more than 300 kgs of potato chips per hour, and the manufacturer is required to pack them in small pouches of 50 gms, 100 gms, etc. Packing machines not only can handle this light weight product of different sizes and shapes of the chip, but with an amazing weighing accuracy of +/–1 chip per pack. The filling machine has several spouts that hold the potato chips to be packed, but the discharge, or filling, takes place only from a few select spouts that are decided by a computer, which calculates the correct combination of spouts that will yield a weight that is close to the desired weight.

Aseptic packing of perishable liquids in tetrapak is again a unique system, and till recently was the monopoly of a single company. They not only produce machines to pack, but also provide their proprietary packing materials that work on these machines.

There are so many bakery products, confectionery items, butter, cheese, etc., that require wrapping in metallic, or other flexible films, and there are special machines for doing so. There are a number of products which are first packed in bags and then the bags are put in a box. For packing of such products, *cartoning* machines are available, which are completely automatic, i.e. packing of material in bags and putting the bags in a carton and sealing, all three functions are done by a single machine. The fastest cartoning machine can handle up to 300 packs per minute.

The packaging industry has made great strides in achieving high speeds, accuracy of filling, trouble free working of the machines, and reducing manpower. In the progress of the processed food industry, the packaging industry has played a pivotal role.

# 7

# Varieties of Processed Foods

There are thousands of processed foods available all over the world. They can be classified into about fifty broad categories. In India, the food industry is at the developmental stage, but some categories of processed foods have already achieved sizeable volumes. There are a number of giant companies who are looking to diversify into the processed food industry, in view of the changing food habits of Indians, and an increase in the population of working women. At present, the following categories of processed foods are widely available in India.

## BAKERY PRODUCTS

Baked products essentially involve baking operations during manufacturing. They are breads, rolls, biscuits, muffins, pies, pastries, cakes, etc. The ingredients used are wheat flour, maida, sugar, salt, vanaspati and dairy products such as milk powder, butter, condensed milk, etc. Generally flour, water and other ingredients are mixed to form the dough. Depending on the product to be made, leavening agents are mixed in the dough. In case of breads and rolls, yeast is added to ferment the dough, and develop the flavour of the bread before baking. Certain chemicals, when heated, produce carbon dioxide, and they are used in bakery products to provide a uniform cell structure and fluffiness. These changes are required for improving the texture of the product. Products such as breads and cakes have a short shelf life and hence their distribution has to be fast. It is for this reason that there are so many small-scale producers in the bakery market. At present, the total turnover of bakery products is around ₹ 8000 crore per year, almost the same as dairy products.

## DAIRY PRODUCTS

Milk is consumed by human beings since ages. People also knew how to prepare curd and/or yoghurt and cheese in most countries. In India, milk of cows, buffaloes and goats is widely used, but in some countries, milk from other animals is also collected. In the Middle-Eastern countries such as Egypt, camel milk is used. There is always a difference in the composition of milk of different animals, especially in relation to the fat content.

As technology developed, it became possible to produce milk powders (skimmed milk and whole milk), ice creams, cheese, etc. Chilled milk in insulated vans could be transported over long distances and kept for several days. In a dairy plant, it became possible to convert surplus milk into powder, by the process of drum drying or spray drying. The same could be reconstituted into milk by the addition of water, as and when necessary. Technology in this way prevented spoilage, and made it possible to make milk and its products available at distant places when needed. In a way, it helped milk producers as well as consumers. It would not have been possible to have the *white revolution* but for modern technology. Today, India is the second largest milk producing country in the world. It produces 110 million tons of milk per annum and approximately 35 per cent of the milk produced is converted into other products.

## BEVERAGES – (NON-ALCOHOLIC)

Beverages are foods which are consumed in liquid form. Most of the beverages are principally consumed when people pause from work, and like to be refreshed and relaxed. Beverages prepared using coffee, tea, malt, cocoa, etc., have been served hot, or cold, for the last several centuries. Tea and coffee plantations were introduced by the British in India. Both tea and coffee are refreshing due to their caffeine content. Tea is also found to contain antioxidants, which are known to delay the ageing process of the body. India accounts for almost one-third of global tea production. It is produced in four states, namely, Assam, West Bengal, Tamil Nadu and Kerala. Lots of unskilled labour, almost a million are employed in the tea gardens. Typical flavour of tea is developed by the process of fermentation of tea leaves and then drying. The taste of tea varies from place to place, i.e. from garden to garden. It is a challenging job to offer tea with a consistent taste and appearance of the beverage, especially when no food additives such as colour, flavour are permitted. For ensuring consistent taste and appearance, marketers prepare tea blends on the basis of opinions given by professional tea tasters. Professional tasters also evaluate tea for valuation.

The preference for different types of natural teas also varies, and for this reason, there are almost three hundred brands of tea marketed, to cater to the needs of the consumers. In 2011, production of tea is estimated to be to the tune of 990 million kilograms. It is believed that consumption of tea in India is about 700 to 800 grams per capita, per year. Lately, instant tea premixes have come into the market, which requires only addition of water to make the beverage. Such premixes are flavoured with different flavours like elaichi, ginger, masala, etc., and marketed in single serve packings. Also, vending machines have been placed at several locations for serving tea in which tea premixes are used.

Coffee is another important beverage which is consumed in large quantities, though not as much as tea. Coffee consumption is almost 25 to 33 per cent of the total consumption of tea. In most other parts of the world, coffee is used in much more quantites than tea. Coffee originated from Arabia and was introduced in Turkey in 1554, Venice in 1668, France in 1644, England and Vienna in 1650 and North America in 1668. India is exporting coffee and instant coffee mostly to European countries. To reduce the costs, chicory is mixed with coffee.

Malt and cocoa powder drinks fortified with nutrients are marketed by multinationals, and their consumption is estimated to be around ₹ 2,000 crore.

Since the last two decades, instant powder soft drinks have come to the market. They too are fortified with micronutrients, but are different in composition, in relation to other beverages. They are acid containing fruit flavoured drinks, and are served chilled.

Another huge category of beverages are carbonated drinks. Such drinks are made using sugar, food acids, natural or artificial flavours and colours, and carbon dioxide gas is impregnated into the beverage under pressure. The gas causes a tingling effect on the tongue when the drink is consumed which adds to the fun and taste. Carbonated drinks are essentially for fun and for thirst quenching, and do not provide much nutrition. Due to the carbon dioxide gas, their bottling or canning requires high pressure fillers with intricate working. There are bottling plants (outside India) where more than twelve hundred glass bottles per minute (bpm) are filled by a single filler. It is considered as a great technical and engineering achievement. When the filler was first-time commissioned in a bottling plant in Japan during the 1970s, the technical head compared it with the fastest machine gun used in the Vietnam War at that time, which fired only eight hundred bullets per minute.

Although soft drinks per se do not contain any harmful or habit forming additives, they are in the news from time to time not only in India but also in other countries. The objection of experts is that soft drinks provide only empty calories without any other nutrients. As a result it contributes to obesity problems especially in case of children. It is estimated that sales of carbonated drinks is around ₹ 6000 crore in the organized sector and an equal value in the unorganized sector. Demand of carbonated drinks per capita is still very low in India when compared to other developed countries and it will continue to grow in hot countries like India.

## BEVERAGES – (ALCOHOLIC)

Drinks which contain alcohol, i.e. ethyl alcohol are covered in this category. The word alcohol is of Arabian origin. Alcohol means a purified substance. Making of an alcoholic drink, involves the process of distillation, which separates the alcohol from other constituents of the liquid. In other words, alcohol is a purified substance, though it really means separated. The modern distillation process was invented in the twelfth century.

Alcohol is produced by breaking down sugar, i.e. carbohydrates in the absence of oxygen. It is known as an anaerobic condition. The breaking down of sugar is carried out by a microorganism, called yeast. It is a single cell organism like bacteria, but its cell size is larger, and reproduces by a process of budding, i.e. a small bud like structure is created which is separated out by splitting. Yeast is capable of multiplying in acidic conditions, and in the absence of oxygen. This is known as fermentation, where it produces alcohol as a secondary metabolite. Various types of alcoholic drinks are produced using different types of substrates (a substrate is a food for the yeast to grow) which are fermented by yeast, till it cannot multiply and stops producing alcohol. This happens because alcohol becomes toxic for yeast to grow further. Then, the fermented broth is distilled and different fractions of the distillate are collected and blended to make alcoholic drinks.

The strength of the alcohol in the drink is expressed in units of proof. The figure of proof is double than that of the alcoholic content, on a volume to volume basis. In other words, if a product is labelled 80 proof alcohol, it contains 40 per cent alcohol in the product on a volume to volume basis, i.e. 100 ml of drink contains 40 ml of alcohol.

There are many types of whiskies available in the market. Whisky is a distillate which is obtained from a fermented wash of grains (or mixture of grains), that have the traditional taste and aroma associated with whisky. When no less than 51 per cent of grain of one type is used, it can be justified by identifying the product accordingly. Malt whisky is made using malt, i.e. sprouted barley as the major grain in the mash of the grains.

Straight whisky is defined as an alcoholic distillate from a fermented mash of grain, that is distilled at not exceeding 160 proof, and withdrawn from cistern room of the distillery, at not more than 110 and not less than 80 proof.

Scotch whisky is mostly a blend of malt whiskies and grain whiskies. Grain whiskies, which are lighter, account for up to 80 per cent of the mixture today. The smoky flavour of scotch results from the drying of the barley malt over a peat fire (decomposed agriculture waste).

Rum is a distillate from the fermented juice of cane, molasses and other sugarcane by-products and distilled at less than 190 proof.

Gin is a distillate obtained either by distillation from a fermented mash, or the re-distillation of neutral spirits with juniper berries and other aromatic botanicals.

Brandy is a distillate from the fermented grape juice, or wine distilled at less than 140 proof alcohol content.

Liqueurs are cordial flavoured brandies and gins which are made by mixing diluted spirits with fruit juices, fruit extracts and fruit flavours, botanical distillates and extracts, essences of essential oils, syrup and water. The sugar content should not be less than 2.5 per cent weight of the finished liqueur.

Vodka is made from neutral spirits, i.e. pure alcohol treated with activated charcoal to remove odour, taste and colour, if any. In Russia, mainly potatoes are used. The alcohol is treated with activated charcoal. The drink is free from acid, and hence flavour does not develop on ageing.

There are many types of alcoholic drinks containing all kinds of flavours depending on local taste. In India, Goa is famous for *Feni* made using cashew nuts. There is a typical *paan* flavoured liqueur. But, products like whisky, rum, gin, brandy, etc., are almost universally available.

The sale of hard drinks is rigidly regulated and heavily taxed. There are some states where there is prohibition. Unfortunately, hard drinks consumption has created many social evils. Illicit alcoholic drinks are made out of the cheapest and harmful materials, and in unhygienic conditions. Several times they are adulterated by the use of denatured alcohol and by methyl alcohol. Every year, many people lose their eyesights and many people die. Due to the huge money involved, authorities do not act firmly to improve the situation. There is a strong case for production of wine made out of grapes and/or other fruits, and making it available without high taxes. At present, the consumption of wine is only 4.5 ml per capita per annum, whereas it is 63.4 liters in Luxembourg and 56.1 liters in France. This may offer a healthier alternative to people, who cannot afford high priced foreign liquors. At the same time, growers of fruits could also benefit.

Beer is another alcoholic drink which is well received in the market. It contains 6 to 8 per cent alcohol. It is produced by fermenting malt, barley hops, etc. Unlike other alcoholic drinks, beer is carbonated, not only to make it enjoyable, but also for the purpose of preservation.

## FRUITS AND VEGETABLE PRODUCTS

Fruits and vegetables are perishable, and hence to preserve them, they are converted into different forms by dehydration, or preserved by canning or bottling in sugar or salt solutions. There are other fruit products such as jams, jellies, marmalades, squashes, cordials and beverages. Fruit beverages are hot filled or pre/post sterilized. Vegetables are dehydrated, canned or converted into chutneys, pickles, ketchup, sauces, etc. It is estimated that 35 per cent of fruits and vegetables are spoilt before they reach the market. Their processing could save up to ₹ 33000 crore per year. In the last five years, several fruit-based drinks have come on to the market, and have been well received by health conscious consumers. Their market is growing at the rate of 25 to 30 per cent, and they have already touched sales of more than ₹ 600 crore.

## CANDY AND CONFECTIONERY FOODS

This category of products are made of sugar syrups, starches, cocoa product, edible oils and nuts, egg products, fruit products, gelatin, dairy products, nut products, acids, colouring, gums, pectin and flavouring materials.

Most people are fond of sweet products. Using the previously mentioned ingredients, hundreds of products are made in this category. It is assumed by Hindus, that Gods and Goddesses also love sweets, and therefore when a *Bhog* is offered to them in temples, a sweet dish is a must. Lord Ganesha is believed to be fond of *modak*.

Traditionally in India, sweets (*Mithai*) have been used since ages, especially to celebrate happy and/or auspicious occasions. These sweets are made out of *khoya* (milk is boiled till it reaches a fat content of at least 30 per cent) along with sugar, and other ingredients, natural and artificial flavours and colours etc. Bengali sweets are produced by acidification of milk, to remove the protein fraction. Thereafter, it is mixed with sugar and other ingredients. All such traditional sweets have a limited shelf life, and hence they are made at the local level. Other types of traditional sweet items are *chikki*, *gachak*, *revadi*, etc., but in their present forms their commercial production on a large-scale offers technical problems.

The most widely available products are hard-boiled candies and chocolate confectionery. Hard-boiled candies are made out of sugar and liquid glucose and contain food acids, flavours, colours, etc. Many hard-boiled candies, chewing gums and chocolate-based confectionary items are of foreign origin. Unlike Indian sweets, they are produced by using machines. They have longer shelf lives, and are properly packed, and can easily be transported.

In the chocolate confectionery category, multinational companies dominate, because of their expertise and sophisticated production facilities. They are marketing various types of chocolates such as milk chocolates, chocolates with centre fillings, etc. They are also promoting consumption on the basis of celebrating a happy occasion, and by projecting chocolate-based confectionary as a snack food.

## SNACK FOODS

Snacks are consumed between meals, and people in India are known to be *snackers*. Traditional snacks are freshly prepared, and mostly served hot, e.g. *idli, dosa* and *upma* in south India, *samosa, kachori, tikkia*, etc., in north and east India and *bhajia, gota, fafda* and *khaman dhokla*, etc., in western India. There is however a big change in the consumption pattern of snacks in the last two decades. Now relatively healthy, tasty and properly packed snacks are easily available at affordable prices. This has impacted the habits of people. These products are produced using modern technology, and special purpose machinery and equipment, such as extruders. Processed snack foods are the fastest-growing category in India, and will continue to grow. Another form of snack food known as *food bar* is still not known to the people in India, but has a huge potential. Such products possess a number of essential characteristics, which adapt them for convenient use under the limitations of time, space and/or the absence of cooking facilities and cleaning facilities.

## HEALTH FOODS

There is a direct relationship between the foods you consume and your health. In spite of knowing this fact, many people cannot resist the temptation of overeating and eating the wrong foods. To address such problems, food processors have adopted a three pronged approach:

1. *To modify existing traditional foods and make them healthier.* In case of sugar containing products, sugar is replaced by non-nutritive sugars, or artificial sweeteners, such as saccharine, aspartame, sucralose, etc. Also fat substitutes are available, and it is now possible to reduce fat content without compromising on the taste, or texture. For example, ice cream is now available containing reduced fat and calories. Sugar has been replaced from carbonated drinks

for the calorie conscious. It is however not so simple to replace sugar by artificial sweeteners. As stated earlier, common sugar has many other functions in a product, in addition to providing sweetness (refer Table 4 and Table 5) Also, their behaviour on the tongue is not the same in terms of response time, for maximum intensity, lingering effect etc. The formulator has to use a blend of sweeteners to overcome these problems, and match the taste of sugar containing products.

2. *To enrich or fortify foods to improve nutritional values.* These foods are diet supplements in a way. Typically, foods are fortified with micronutrients such as vitamins and minerals. Common salt available is fortified with iodine. Sometimes, flour or attas are also fortified with vitamins. Many a time processed food manufacturers are fortifying their products. All such products are required to give information about their nutrient contents on the back of the pack.

3. *To design functional foods.* A functional food is specifically designed to address a specific medical condition. There is a growing need for functional foods to address obesity, cardiovascular health, diabetes, bone health, cognitive functions, digestive health, eye health, stress and fatigue, insomnia, and anti-aging among others. In all such products, specific bioactive material(s) that are known to have specific health benefits are incorporated in the food items. The food items chosen, are the ones that are consumed regularly, since this ensures better compliance. Mostly, functional foods are sold in beverage form, or in the form of food bars. There is even an approach to enhance the quality of water, by mixing micronutrients in it. These micronutrients are packed in a specially designed pack called stick pack and the contents of the pack are meant to be mixed in regular water bottles that are sold in the market. This concept has caught on in the USA, and soon we may have such products available in the Indian market.

> The total sales of functional foods and beverages reached US$ 37.4 billion in 2009 in the USA of which US$ 21.6 billion sales was of beverages alone. In other words, functional foods in beverage forms are more acceptable.

Each category of functional foods requires expertise in not just selecting bioactive materials, but also their incorporation in the product. Functional foods are also known as *nutraceuticals,* since these products act like pharmaceuticals, offering health benefits, but sold as food products. Experts believe that the business of nutraceuticals will outperform sales of pharmaceutical preparations in a few years.

Of all the functional foods, products related to weight management are front runners. Obesity is considered to be the number one health problem in the United States, and in India too, it is a serious problem amongst well-to-do people. Obesity not only affects the appearance of a person, but also reduces his fitness, and leads to other health problems such as diabetes, cardiovascular diseases, etc. Although people are aware of this, and also dietary guidelines are given by experts, but the fact is, that the problem of obesity is on the rise with modern lifestyles. People who design products for weight management, not only use their knowledge of reduction of calories, but also know how to address the problem of satiety (feeling of fullness in the stomach), without compromising on the enjoyment part of the food. Another important category of functional foods is for the management of diabetes. Diabetes cannot be cured, but it can be controlled, and functional foods could play a vital role for keeping diabetes in check. These foods are designed to prevent spikes in the glucose levels by slowing down the discharge of food from the stomach to the intestine – where sugar gets absorbed into the blood. Fenugreek fibres derived by a patented process are found to work on this principle. There are foods which are designed to improve resistance to insulin. For example, certain chromium salts are found to promote insulin sensitivity. Polyphenols of cinnamon, olive extracts, black tea, blueberries, etc., are also found to prevent increase in the level of glucose in

Type II diabetes. Consumption of whole grains and fruits and vegetables having fibre and plant cell materials also help as they make starchy food physically inaccessible to the enzyme responsible for starch digestion. This also helps in weight management.

Functional foods for heart care are designed to improve the lipid profile. Fibre containing products help in reducing cholesterol and also in improving digestive health. Fibre serves as a prebiotic and supports growth of good micro-organisms in the gut. Inulin is a type of fibre that is reported to improve the absorption of calcium which is required for bone health For knee joints, foods enriched with glucosamine and condroitin sulphate are found to be effective, since they help in the regeneration of the cartilage of the joint. Functional foods for boosting beauty will also be in the market. There are ingredients which are supposed to work on the skin not externally, but from within. There are functional foods rich in antioxidants that slow the process of ageing. As our knowledge about substances and disease relationships expands, more and more functional foods would come into the market. So far, in India, functional foods are not widely available and popular, but there is an urgent need to have an experts committee to approve health claims made about a substance and its relationship with a disease. In the US, the FDAMA (Food and Drug Administration Modernization Act) permits the use of health or nutrient content claims based on currently published authoritative statements from certain federal scientific bodies, and the National Academy of Sciences. At present, in India, there are several companies that are making health claims, not just on their labels, but also in their advertisements in the print and TV media. The Horlicks commercial on the lines of *'Taller, Stronger, Sharper'* was not permitted in UK, as reported, whereas the company continued to run this advertisement in India. They also ran advertisements telling students *'Exams Ke Bhoot Bhagao'* by drinking two cups of Horlicks everyday. The competitor Complan also tells parents of the students for providing *'Complan Memory'* to their children thus indirectly making parents guilty for poor performance of their children. There is an urgent need to have an authority to look into these types of claims to validate them.

India has deep knowledge of *Ayurveda* and herbal medicines. If these could be tested properly for bioactive materials by using modern scientific methods, there could be several substances that could be identified for the development of functional foods. Such products will have a huge market, not just in India, but throughout the world. For example, India is exporting psyllium husk-based product in large quantities from Gujarat. Similar opportunities exist for a number of typical Indian herbs.

The following Tables 7.1 and Table 7.2 give details of health claims and nutrient content claims of labels of processed, packaged foods available in the USA. In India too, similar declarations have started appearing on processed foods.

**Table 7.1:** Percentage of Products Within Product Groups with Health Claims and Qualified Health Claims (Courtesy: Food Label and Package Survey 2006-2007)

| *Product Group* | *% of Products Sold with Health Claims* | *Subject of Health Claims and Qualified Health Claims Used (Examples)* |
|---|---|---|
| Nuts | 46.6 | Nuts and coronary heart disease (CHD)<br>Walnut and CHD |
| Cereals – cold | 43.4 | Dietary saturated fat and cholesterol and CHD<br>Soluble fibre from certain foods and CHD<br>Whole grains and CHD<br>Fruits, vegetables and grain products that contain<br>fibre and CHD<br>Potassium and sodium and blood pressure |
| Cereals – hot | 38.4 | Soluble fibre from certain foods and CHD<br>Dietary saturated fat and cholesterol and CHD<br>Whole grain and CHD |

| *Product Group* | *% of Products Sold with Health Claims* | *Subject of Health Claims and Qualified Health Claims Used (Examples)* |
|---|---|---|
| Beverages – other dairy | 35.9 | Soy protein and CHD |
| Vegetable and grains – Dried | 17.5 | Dietary saturated fat and cholesterol and CHD |
| Seafood – canned and Frozen | 15.0 | Dietary saturated fat and cholesterol and CHD |
| Baking mixes | 10.1 | Dietary saturated fat and cholesterol and CHD |
| Crackers | 10.0 | Whole grains and CHD<br>Whole grains and CHD and certain cancers |
| Fresh and shelf-stable breads and baked goods | 8.6 | Whole grains and CHD and other cancers<br>Dietary saturated fat and cholesterol<br>Dietary lipids (fat) and cancer |
| Pasta | 7.9 | Dietary saturated fat and cholesterol and CHD |

**Table 7.2:** Percentages of Products with Select Nutrient Content Claims
(Courtesy: Food Label and Package Survey 2006-2007)

| *Type of Claim* | *% of Products Sold with Claims* | *Top 5 Product Groups with Claims* | *% of Product Group* |
|---|---|---|---|
| Calorie-related claims (Calorie free, Low or reduced calorie) | 10.3 | Sugar and sugar substitutes<br>Butters, margarines, and spreads<br>Cereals – cold<br>Beverages – carbonated soft drinks<br>Puddings, gelatins, toppings, fillings, and syrups | 46.2<br>36.3<br>36.1<br>35.1<br>31.1 |

| *Type of Claim* | *% of Products Sold with Claims* | *Top 5 Product Groups with Claims* | *% of Product Group* |
|---|---|---|---|
| Fat claims (Fat free, Low or reduced fat %) | 22.4 | Milk<br>Cereals – hot<br>Dried vegetables and grains<br>Fruit – dried, fresh and frozen<br>Miscellaneous dairy | 92.6<br>84.3<br>82.5<br>65.9<br>65.0 |
| Saturated fat claims (Saturated fat free, low or reduced Saturated fat) | 3.6 | Meat and poultry substitutes<br>Crackers<br>Butter, margarines and spreads<br>Shortenings and oils<br>Salad dressings and toppings | 49.5<br>42.3<br>27.5<br>26.0<br>19.9 |
| Cholesterol claims (Cholesterol free, low or reduced cholesterol | 6.9 | Hot cereals<br>Crackers<br>Meat/poultry substitutes<br>Butter, margarines and spreads<br>Beverages – other dairy drinks and substitutes | 64.5<br>54.6<br>49.5<br>36.3<br>35.9 |
| Sodium claims (Sodium free, low or reduced sodium no added salt, salt free, lightly salted) | 7.5 | Beverages – carbonated soft drinks<br>Dried vegetables and grains<br>Beverages – dairy and non-dairy Beverages/mixes<br>Nuts and seeds<br>Pasta | 57.6<br>52.4<br>42.9<br>26.1<br>23.8 |
| Fibre related claims (Excellent or good source of fibre, more fibre) | 3.1 | Cereals – cold<br>Cereals – hot<br>Crackers<br>Soups<br>Fruits – dried, fresh and frozen | 29.0<br>23.7<br>13.2<br>12.1<br>10.6 |

| Type of Claim | % of Products Sold with Claims | Top 5 Product Groups with Claims | % of Product Group |
|---|---|---|---|
| Sugar claims (Sugar free, reduced sugar, no added sugar unsweetened) | 4.5 | Beverages – dairy and non-dairy beverages/mixes<br>Puddings – gelatins, toppings, fillings and syrups<br>Beverages – juices/drinks-refrigerated and shelf stable<br>Beverages-carbonated soft drinks<br>Candies – non-chocolate | 42.9<br>30.2<br>15.2<br>13.3<br>11.1 |

# 8

# Marketing of Processed Foods

Marketing of Fast Moving Consumer Goods (FMCG) products is always a challenging job, especially for food products. It requires not only resources to create awareness, and organize distribution, but also requires understanding of potential customers' responses in terms of acceptance, or rejection of the product for reasons that are sometimes unpredictable. A gentleman named Peryam, who worked with the US army in Chicago stated:

> *Food is for people, and their reactions to it are important. Taste, odour, texture, consistency and the like, are considered to be properties of food, but perhaps it is more valid to look on them as properties of peoples' behaviour towards food. These properties arise from physical and chemical stimuli, but stimuli are not the properties. Furthermore, interest is usually focused not on description, but on user acceptance or preference. In such cases we are dealing with people properties and not food properties.*
>
> *Different people give different responses to the same quality of food properties due to physiological reasons. Physiology of taste and odour senses is not identical in the case of all the consumers. Likes and dislikes of a food product depends mainly on taste and odour perception of a consumer. Although to some extent, other senses too play some role in acceptance or rejection. Appearance and texture,*

*i.e. mouth feel, are also important. A negative remark could also develop prejudice and influence opinion of the other person.*

Let us understand how the tongue and nose perceive taste and smell sensations.

There are thousands of taste receptors on the tongue, and millions of olfactory receptors in the nose. They are physiologically known as neurons, i.e. having nerve fibres to convey information to the brain. The taste cells are located in the taste buds which are present in finger like projections distributed over the tongue. There are several thousand taste buds and each taste bud contains 8-10 cells. It has been seen that the sweet taste is most readily sensed at the tip of the tongue, a sour taste at the edge of the tongue, and a salty taste along the tip and edges. Bitter food is tasted at the end of the tongue. As a result, if a solution containing sweet and bitter components is placed in the mouth, we taste the sweet before the bitter, and the bitter lingers, after the sweet has vanished. Discrimination between tastes therefore is, in part, recognition of these spatial and temporal patterns. Physiologists have tried to study by electro-physiological methods, the behaviour of the taste cells in case of human beings and mammals, and have found marked differences in the behaviour to stimulants. Stimulants are chemicals present in food and they are less than 0.2 per cent of the weight of the food. All the cells do not have an identical behaviour, even if they are located in the same taste bud. Also, it was found that a single taste cell could respond to more than one taste quality. Simultaneously, nerve activity is taking place in the olfactory cells of the nose from the volatile chemicals emitted from food. Therefore, it is the total pattern of nerve activity coming from many taste cells and olfactory cells, that determines the perceived taste quality. Combined activities, or signals are conveyed to the brain. These signals are processed in our mind, which then decides about the likes and dislikes, i.e. acceptance, or rejection, on the basis of information stored earlier. As explained earlier, it is unlikely that two persons can have identical sensations due to the spatial and temporal patterns involved. Though there could be similarities in the pattern of likes or dislikes.

There is another important physiological aspect regarding acceptance or rejection of author food. Many foods when consumed for the first time are not accepted. When the author went to the USA for studies for the first time, initially he didn't like cheese, beer and soya products. However, on repeated consumption he acquired a taste for products such as pizza, spaghetti, etc. Over a period, he not only accepted the taste, but started relishing these products.

The following is an interesting example of a physiologically acquired taste in the case of animals.

In the past, when molasses-based cattle feed was introduced by a company in India, the same was rejected by the animals. The company never imagined that animals could also have likes and dislikes. They were used to the taste of cotton seeds and other cereals. It was not so easy to introduce molasses in the animal food formula, which they wanted to do, for economic and technical reasons. Management was worried, but in the same year that the product was launched, there was a severe drought and farmers made animals forcibly consume the feed. The result was that the animals not only acquired a taste for molasses, but also developed a preference for the taste. After conditions became normal, the animals did not accept cotton seeds and other materials to which they were used to earlier.

In another instance, a well-known pharmaceutical company which introduced a vitamin mix for use in cattle feed, faced problems of non-acceptance, in spite of prolonged trials. Nobody thought that a small quantity of vitamin mix in animal feed could make such a difference. The author, being a flavour manufacturer was then contacted for solutions, and he developed a suitable flavour based on a similar imported sample. The small quantity of flavour worked wonders. The veterinary doctor of the company carried out trials on animals by offering feed containing flavour and without flavour. In a shed, several animals were served feed at the same time, and in the trial experiment, alternate animals were served flavoured feed, and the one next to it was served without flavour. What followed was a commotion – in the words of the doctor. The animal which did not receive flavoured feed could perceive the difference in the feed consumed by the neighbouring animal, and it tried to push that animal away so as to have the flavoured feed.

Many times, once a person is used to a particular taste, he would not prefer any change even if it is better. In 1985, a world renowned cola soft drink manufacturer announced that it would alter its formulation and offer a better tasting product that was developed based on the feedback of almost two hundred thousand people. The study had revealed a resounding preference for the new product, and the company decided with tremendous confidence and enthusiasm, to introduce the bold change. The reaction of the American people was immediate and violent, and within a period of three months, the company had to reintroduce the original product. The entire episode is viewed differently by different people. Some people view it as a huge publicity stunt, designed to launch a new cola, and boost the sales of the old one.

It has been established that children are more adaptive and flexible in trying out different products. In India, in the past, people of south India were rice eaters and did not consume wheat preparations. For this reason, there were not many bread manufacturing units in south India. But, to meet shortages of rice and to popularize bread, a public sector enterprise started manufacturing bread in south India, even at the risk of making losses. As a result, today young people in south India, have accepted bread, and similarly, south Indian restaurants have made *idli* and *dosa* popular throughout India. In a way, food habits are changing due to several reasons. This is also true in many other countries. In the US, a large number of people are exposed to ethnic products of other countries, and have started liking hot and savoury products. In the UK also, people have developed preferences for the *curry* taste. Food manufacturers have to constantly be in touch with changing food habits. Of course, food habits are hard to change, and therefore food companies are targeting young children, so that they develop a taste for their product from the beginning, and remain customers for a long time.

Another important aspect is highlighted, related to food consumption. Once a person develops a liking for a particular food, he develops a strong desire to have it again and again. Universally, people have a weakness for food. This weakness prevails amongst people of all regions, young or old, rich or poor, men or women, etc. A very interesting article appeared sometime back in *The Indian Express* by Saritha Rai – 'The Food Court Rules'. In leading IT companies at Bangalore, the employees consume rich, generous foods in the cafeterias that is heavily subsidized by the employers. It is not quantity alone, but the quality of foods that has created problems of obesity, and have made the employees sluggish and victims of lifestyle diseases. A leading IT company decided to experiment with a parallel healthy menu by substituting *paranthas* with *phulkas, biryani* with plain rice and *dals*, desserts with fruits and offering two vegetables and curd and buttermilk. In the beginning, the healthy menu counters averaged 300 takers from amongst thousands of employees and after a few weeks it dropped to a steady 150 employees. People cannot resist being tempted for consuming foods of their choice. It also proves that people prefer taste to health.

During the author's long association with the food industry, he saw many products which failed miserably in the market soon after being launched. In all such cases, due importance was not given to the previously discussed aspects of food acceptance. All people involved were successful business people, but in different fields like chemical manufacturing, pharmaceuticals manufacturing, garments, etc. The management went by their personal choices and ignored the opinion of professionals.

A well-known pharmaceutical company marketed a protein food product using soy flour, cocoa powder and sugar. The product was sold as an over the counter (OTC) product, but it was not accepted, because it had an awful beany taste. The management was overconfident, and assumed that any product with their brand name would sell.

Another company manufacturing soya oil marketed flavoured soya milk in tetrapaks which also was rejected.

In case of potato chips, a manufacturer launched chips and made them look white, unlike a regular product which is more brownish. He did not realize that the process of removing the brown colour results in loss of the potato taste in the product. The market rejected the product, because it was colourless and tasteless.

A snack food company in Madhya Pradesh made huge investments in a snack food plant, and launched a product that had a meaty taste. In Madhya Pradesh, a large part of the population is vegetarian. A similar product having a meaty taste was very popular in Germany. The author developed seasonings having a meaty taste which the management approved, and also offered a masala type seasoning and prepared samples of the final product. The marketing people were very happy since the product had an Indianized taste. However, the promoters did not care to listen. One of the partners was German, and he too felt that the local taste must be given preference. His opinion was also overruled. The product bombed very badly once it was launched. Today, a world leader in snack food business has marketed similar snack foods with masala seasonings that suit local tastes and they have achieved a huge success.

A hard-boiled candy manufacturer for the first time in India marketed hard boiled candy with artificial hard drink flavour such as whisky, rum, gin, etc. He declared on the packing *'Contains zero per cent alcohol'*. Hard drinks are consumed not because of the taste, but because of their alcohol content. Children did not accept the unfamiliar taste of hard drinks. The company also had problems with authorities, and this led to closure of their operations.

A well-known soft drinks company marketed a grape flavoured drink in the 1970s assuming that the brand name would sell. Most consumers complained about the medicinal taste and never tried the product again. The same product was extremely popular in Japan at that time. Grape as a taste, is now gaining acceptance in the Indian market. This seems to be a case of acquired taste.

There could be a very long list of products but only a few examples have been given of products where money and marketing was not a problem, and products were manufactured in modern facilities, but still failed. In most cases mentioned earlier, the management was overconfident and secretive about their products and did not think of carrying out any consumer preference studies. It is imperative to make sure of acceptance of products before being launched in the market.

A systematic consumer preference test as described now, needs to be carried out before the launch of a product.

*Pair* test is a must, by comparing the new product to a competitor's product, in cases where it is available. One has to make sure that the product is at least equal, or better. In case the product is different, and no comparative product is available the *Absolute* judgement test is carried out. In case of the pair test, and in case of the absolute judgement test, simple questions are posed. In case of the pair test, two samples with code numbers are given, and opinions solicited to find out which is better. In case of the absolute judgement test, the sample is to be rated on a hedonic scale by the respondent. Typically, a respondent is asked to give ratings by commenting as follows:

I like the sample extremely

I like the sample very much

I do not like nor dislike.

I dislike very much

I dislike extremely

Also comments are solicited about what you like or what you do not like.

Selection of respondents is very important and care must be taken to select a cross-section that would be representative potential consumers. The answers are subjected to statistical analysis, and decisions taken by ensuring at least 95 per cent confidence levels in the new product. If adverse comments are made, they should be thoroughly examined and possible remedial measures taken.

Another important issue is the shelf life of food products. Shelf life varies from product to product. Products such as bread has a shelf life of a few hours, whereas some products have shelf lives of more than a year. It is important that product stays almost factory fresh as far as possible, till it is consumed. In India, marketing conditions are harsh compared to other countries, due to high temperatures and high humidity. In the developed world, most of the retail shops are air-conditioned, or if not then at least they have some temperature and humidity control. In India, leaving aside the modern retail format, a majority of the shops are exposed to high temperatures. Storage of food products at elevated temperatures and at high humidity affects their shelf life considerably. Many times products are stacked outside the shop, due to lack of space inside, thus exposing them to direct sunlight. In general, products get abused not only due to high temperatures and humidity, but also due to rough roads, exposure of product to direct sunlight, and rough handling of packages by transporters. At retails outlets, especially in rural areas, and in godowns, rodents play havoc. A product – a chocolate flavoured milk packed in a tetrapak faced severe problems due to rodent bites making the product leak, thereby affecting sterility of the product. Also, leakage of the product spoiled other containers packed in the same package.

More and more products are marketed that contain nutrients, such as vitamins and minerals. There are many vitamins which cannot take such abuse. Keeping this in mind, suppliers of vitamin premixes add on extra quantity of vitamins, based on their experiences. Extra addition is not only expensive, but at times it also affects taste. Many manufacturers are not even aware of the fact that vitamins get degraded during storage, and in such cases the consumer is not getting the dosage of vitamins as advertised, or mentioned on labels.

Generally shelf life studies are carried out in a laboratory, prior to launching of the product, but most of the times management is always in a hurry to market the product without proper shelf life studies. Also, due to the prevailing trade practices, a company is keen to declare maximum shelf life. This is due to fear of goods being returned by the retailers. In developed countries, processed foods are consumed within less than a month's time from the date of manufacture, or once put on retail shelves. In Indian conditions, many products remain unsold even after 12 months. This situation arises due to various reasons. Sometimes, it is due to lack of demand. In other cases, products get dumped into the market by force by the sales teams of large FMCG companies, since they have to meet their sales targets. Sometimes, large quantities are pushed to distributors, or retailers, by giving them incentives. In the interests of the consumers, and for the reputation of the company, such practices should be avoided.

In addition, there are other important marketing aspects, which are similar to the marketing of other FMCG products. One needs to study the market in terms of the size of the market, competitors, price structures, distribution network, positive and negative attributes of competitor's products, etc. Based on this information one has to design its USP, i.e. *Unique Sales Proposition* of the product to be marketed. In other words, why should a consumer buy your product? In case of food products, the USP could be in terms of taste and appearance, packaging, price, health benefits, etc.

India is a huge market for consumer products, because after economic reforms were introduced twenty years ago, there is an increase in the middle-class population. Purchasing power has increased considerably, which can be seen by the increase in sales of many consumer products and consumer durable products. The market is like a pyramid representing various sections of society. Marketing experts decide to position products aiming at specific sections of society, on the basis of potential customers. To illustrate the point, an example is now given of a product just recently introduced.

Malt-based beverages have been in India for a long time and are very popular and considered as a huge category of products. There are only a few giant multinational companies marketing them. The products marketed by them are designed for children from a nutritional perspective. These products command tremendous brand loyalty, and consumers who have been using these products when they were children, continue to consume them even after they have grown up, although the product offers no nutritional benefits for adults. The new entrant saw an opportunity in this, and developed a malt-based beverage, similar to the products from multinationals, but with nutrients, keeping in mind the nutritional needs of adults. The product's USP and positioning is clearly seen in their advertisement, in which a child is questioning his father on the breakfast table – 'Why are you drinking my drink?' The product is clearly positioned for well-to-do adults, and its USP is 'Nutrition for adults' to differentiate it from the regular product.

Another example is of a product, which is positioned to serve the masses – consumers who are at the bottom of the pyramid. One of our customers has a wide distribution network at the low end of the market, such as *paan waalas, laari galas*, etc., marketing tobacco products. The customer approached the author for a powder instant drink to be marketed at the MRP of ₹ 1 per serving. The consumer is required to add only water to the powder, which makes an effervescent drink. The product became a huge success immediately on introduction, even though it was hardly advertised. In the African continent, extremely cheap powder drink products are marketed, and there is a huge demand for such products. Nowadays even large food companies, including multinationals, have started paying attention to the needs of the people at the bottom of the pyramid.

The marketplace is like a battlefield. In order to be successful, one has to be good in strategy planning. Many new entrants in the market have faced unexpected problems created by competition, who wanted to kill the new companies or products, so that they would not become a threat in the future. Three decades ago, the author faced a serious problem, when he started his manufacturing unit. A multinational, making the same products, tried to undercut prices and offered their products below cost to our potential customers. They were in a position to do this, since they were large, and could afford to lose some money. They were making huge profits from other clients. It became very difficult for the author to explain the situation to his customers, and the only way to overcome the problem was by proving that his products were superior to the multinational's products by getting them evaluated by a consumer preference study carried out by independent agencies. The author also offered his product on an exclusive basis to his client which the multinational could not afford. There are so many instances of such unhealthy practices by big companies, including multinationals, not only in food, but across categories. One of the leading Indian manufacturers of washing powder, faced a similar problem, and is a well-known story. In the late fifties, a leading multinational company was marketing milk-based baby foods imported from the UK. They wanted to ensure having a monopoly, by discouraging the use of products locally manufactured in India on the grounds of poor quality of milk available for manufacture in India, and poor hygienic conditions. A leading Indian producer of milk products developed milk-based baby food with the help of Indian scientists, and was ready to go to the market. The multinational tried to ensure that the new product was not accepted by the Indian consumer. They built a huge stock of their own product, while creating short supplies in the market, and decided to flood the market just before the launch of the Indian product. Having come to know of the strategy of the multinational, the management of the Indian company changed their launch plans overnight, and rather than launching the product in the western part of India, launched in south India through a newly appointed distributor, who was very powerful. The multinational could not supply their product in southern India. The new product was well received in the absence of the multinational's product, and proved that there was no quality issue with the Indian product. Later on, the multinational was also forced to manufacture their product in India. At present, milk-based baby foods are not available since breast feeding is the best for infants. Medical practitioners and UNICEF have very effectively reduced the consumption of baby foods.

It is not always that new entrants have to face trouble from well-established competitors. When a new entrant has a better product, a smart marketing strategy and money power, he will make well-established brands almost disappear. In the fifties, a well-known brand of butter was not able to face competition against a new entrant, who today has become a well-known leader in the market. It was not so difficult for the new company to successfully eliminate the competitor's brand, as the product – butter was a commodity, and it did not involve much technology. The same company was not successful in the case of other sophisticated products, such as chocolates and malt beverages.

In the seventies, soft drinks were marketed only in glass bottles. Empty bottles were collected from the market and recycled for production. A new company marked out a very clever strategy before launching its new orange flavoured drink. They quietly started collecting empties of the competitors from the trade, and sent them away to far away territories of another franchisee of the same drink at discounted prices. Hence, when the new product was launched in his territory, the local competitor was unable to supply his product, since he did not have any empties for bottling. Also, the new product was a superior product and was well received, in the absence of the established product.

Many new products keep coming out in the marketplace, but not all of them survive. The new product has to find, or create its place in the market. It is like *'everything is fair in love and war'*. Once the new product is accepted by consumers, sales will grow fast. Food products enjoy repeat sales, and many times, they are purchased through impulse buying. Because of this, the product should be made available everywhere. This is often called as being available at an arm's length of desire. This means the product should be so well distributed that it should be only an arm's length away, should a consumer have the impulse to consume it. Food products should also be well displayed at the point of sale.

Just as the army needs the support of the air force for striking enemies, the sales people need the support of advertisements.

Advertisements not only create awareness, but also generate interest in the product. They create a pull to attract consumers. At the time of the launch, the market is bombarded with advertisements, and once the product has started moving, advertisements are reduced, but never stopped. An expert on advertising says that 50 per cent of ad expenses are wasteful, but unfortunately we do not know which 50 per cent works. Today, ads on TV are the most expensive, but viewers flick channels as soon as advertisements appear. Many food companies push their sales by giving incentives not only to consumers, but also to retailers. Retailers work as opinion formers, and try to influence consumer decisions. It is important to make the consumer taste the product. Sampling can be carried out in many ways in public places, or at homes. Many food companies encourage visits to their factories in groups. Such visits create long-lasting favourable impressions in the minds of the consumers, and eliminate doubts regarding quality issues. The most preferred visitors are school children, and women's groups. They are also given mementoes with the logo of the brand name. These visitors not only are the decision makers, but they also talk to others about their visit. They help in promoting the brand through word of mouth publicity. All such efforts help in creating brand image and brand loyalty.

At present, the total size of the Indian food industry is around US $250 billion of which only about 20 per cent is accounted for by value added food products. Value added products are all kinds of beverages, soft drinks, packaged water, bakery products, ready to cook and ready to serve products, dairy products, etc. The growth of the food industry will depend on the economic development of the country. Poor people live mainly on staple foods, and if their incomes improve, their priority will be for dairy, meat, vegetable oils, sugar, vegetables, etc. In other words, they will increase the consumption of commodities. In the case of middle-class of people, they look for convenience foods. The reason is because more and more women will be working, yet they would still like to cook the food for their family members. They would like to cook traditional foods but with lesser efforts. They would go out and eat once in a while, and try different foods. The upper class of people will eat out more often, because of social and business reasons. But, due to their lifestyles, they would prefer to consume at home, diet foods, functional foods, organic foods and healthier versions of traditional foods. The most liked traditional foods are made with sugar, vegetable oils, vanaspati, etc. Their healthier versions could be made by replacing sugar with artificial sweeteners and by replacing fats with fat substitutes. Unfortunately, traditional and ethnic products are not mass produced in the organized sector, and people who are engaged in making such products, are not technically sound to develop such products. As such, for the mass production of typical Indian products, there is hardly any developmental work on the machinery and equipment. Most of the value added products made in India, are manufactured using machinery and equipment originally designed and developed in foreign countries for their products. Lately, products such as *papad*, *khakra* made out of *chappati*, and a few namkeen items, etc., are being made using simple machines such as the *atta* mixer, roller, baking oven, fryer, etc. They are also packed using simple vacuum sealers.

There are good possibilities of our government permitting FDI in multi-product retail chains. If Wal-Mart and other multinational retail chains come to the Indian market they would impact the food business scenario. They may encourage small but competent manufacturers, and market products under their store brands. Also they would export some of these products to their outlets in other countries.

# 9

# Nutrition and Lifestyle Diseases

Any living organism requires food for growth and for living. For living, the energy required is provided by the foods, of which the original source is sunlight. Plants, algae and some species of bacteria are capable of using sunlight to fix carbon dioxide and water, by a process called photosynthesis. This process produces different types of sugars (carbohydrates) which are further converted into fats, proteins and other micro-nutrients such as vitamins. Keeping in view the requirements of the reader, the details of the chemical structure and other related aspects of nutrients, are not discussed in this book. The information given in this chapter is of a general nature, but useful, so as to enable the reader to decide on a proper choice of food. Recent changes in food laws have made it mandatory for food processors to give basic nutritional information on the pack, so that the consumer knows what he is consuming. However, a consumer should have basic knowledge of nutrition, to appreciate the information given on the pack.

## CARBOHYDRATES

Carbohydrates accumulate, or store energy, when they are synthesized by photosynthesis, and when they are broken down in the body this energy gets released. The process of photosynthesis and breaking down of carbohydrates are carried out by biochemical reactions. Biochemical reactions are chemical reactions carried out in living systems. Unlike chemical reactions, biochemical reactions are silently taking place at relatively low temperatures in the presence of body catalysts, called enzymes. In living systems, there are several enzymes, and each enzyme has a specific function to perform in the biochemical reaction taking place. All enzymes are proteins. They are capable of lowering the requirements of energy for carrying out a reaction. For example, if starch is to be broken down by a chemical reaction in a laboratory, it needs to be heated with hydrochloric acid for several hours, whereas the same starch molecule can be broken down just by adding saliva from our mouth. An enzyme *amylase* present in the saliva does the same job at room temperature almost instantly. At present, a number of enzymes are commercially produced, and they are used for various purposes. They are employed in the food and pharmaceutical industries, effluent disposal, detergents/washing compounds, etc. The pathways of biochemical reactions that occur during the breaking down of carbohydrates are well-known to a biochemist. Carbohydrates are broken down into a six carbon atom sugar, known as *glucose*, which goes through a burning process in the body cells. After complete burning, carbon dioxide gas is produced which is exhaled into the atmosphere. The burning process is carried out in a series of biochemical reactions knocking out the carbon atoms, one by one. Every time a carbon atom is knocked out, energy is released. The burning of the initial three carbon atoms can be carried out without involving oxygen, and for the remaining three carbon atoms the presence of oxygen is necessary. The first half of the pathway of this breaking down is known as *glycolysis* and the other half is known as the *Krebs cycle* named after Hans Krebs, a German biochemist, who discovered this pathway and was awarded the Nobel Prize for his work.

Carbohydrates are complex chemicals made of carbon, hydrogen and oxygen. Normally, they are polymers of sugar. For example, starch is a polymer of glucose. Before carbohydrates begin the burning process, they need to be broken into the glucose molecule, by an enzyme called amylase.

From the nutrition point of view, all carbohydrates give 4.0 calories (kcal) per gram. Nutrition experts recommend that approximately 55 per cent of total calories consumed in a day, should come from carbohydrates. The most important issue related to carbohydrates is a disease called diabetes. In the diabetic condition, the glucose levels in the blood rise above the normal limit leading to many physiological conditions, which over a period affect the kidneys, eyes, heart, etc. In the case of a normal person, the glucose levels are maintained within the range of 70 to 110 mg/dl, but when food is consumed, it gets absorbed into the blood from the intestine. The blood sugar levels then rise from 110mg/dl and could go beyond 300 to 400 mg/dl. At that stage a hormone produced by the pancreas known as insulin is secreted. It starts working to reduce the level of glucose by facilitating the absorption of glucose from blood in the body cells for burning. In the case of a healthy person, the sugar levels are brought within the normal range within two hours. In case, if blood sugar falls below 70 mg/dl, sugar is released from the liver to increase its level back to within the normal range. There are two types of diabetes, namely Type I and Type II. In case of Type I diabetes, people are born with a defect in their pancreas, which results in their being unable to produce insulin, whereas in Type II diabetes, people develop resistance to the action of insulin, and insulin secretion cannot be increased by the pancreas to the extent required to maintain the sugar levels within the normal range. In order for diabetes to develop, both insulin secretion and insulin sensitivity (ability to lower sugar) have to be impaired. For the treatment of diabetes, oral medicines are given that reduce the resistance to the action of insulin or stimulate secretion of insulin in patients. Alternately, an extra quantity of insulin is injected in the patients. There are a variety of oral drugs and insulins such as fast acting, slow acting, etc. Depending on individual needs of the patient, doctors choose suitable medication or combinations thereof, to manage diabetes. It is possible to control diabetes by a proper diet, medications and by living a disciplined life. People with diabetes can live the full span of life if their diabetes is managed effectively.

To determine the potential risk, or a stage before development of diabetes, the glucose tolerance test is done. In this test, an individual is asked to fast overnight (8-12 hours) and then given a glucose solution (75 g). Blood samples are drawn before serving, and at various time intervals (typically after two hours) and tested for blood glucose levels. Soon after serving the sample, the blood glucose level will peak to the maximum, and in the case of a healthy person, the level should come back down to the initial level within two hours. In case the time taken is more than two hours it indicates conditions of impaired glucose tolerance which means that though a person is not yet diabetic, he is facing the risk of developing diabetic conditions. Typically fasting blood glucose levels should be below 100 mg/dL. Fasting levels between 110–125 mg/L are border line cases, and fasting levels repeatedly above 200 mg/dL are indicative of diabetes. Similarly, glucose levels after two hours should be below 140 mg/dL in case of a healthy person. Levels between 140 and 200 mg/dL indicate impaired glucose tolerance, and levels consistently above 200 mg/dL after two hours confirms diagnosis of diabetes. *Once a person is diabetic, he is always diabetic.*

The effect of different foods on blood glucose (sugar) levels over a period of time have been studied, and it is found that some kinds of foods may raise blood glucose levels more quickly than other foods even though both contain the same amounts of carbohydrates (glycaemic load). In other words, some foods get digested more quickly, and hence release glucose into the bloodstream faster than others. This rate of release of glucose into the blood is called their *glycaemic response.*

In order to have a comparative idea of the glycaemic response of different foods, they are assigned a glycaemic index (GI). Carbohydrate foods that break down quickly during digestion, have the highest glycaemic indexes, because their blood sugar response is fast and high. Carbohydrates that break down slowly, releasing glucose gradually into the blood stream, have low glycaemic indexes (GI). Since low GI foods release glucose into the blood stream more slowly, their requirement of insulin is lesser, and hence low GI diets can help people control their diabetes. Loss of weight and physical activities improve the body's sensitivity to insulin. Table 9.1 gives details of the glycaemic index of some common foods:

Experts recommend avoiding spikes in sugar levels and dividing the glycaemic load by consuming food in at least four small meals at regular intervals, instead of consuming a lot of food at a time.

**Table 9.1:** The Glycaemic Index of Some Common Foods (Using Glucose as a Standard. Glucose = 100)

| **Foods with a low G.I. Factor (G.I. less than 55)** |
|---|
| Noodles and pasta |
| Lentils |
| Apples/apples juice |
| Pears |
| Oranges/orange juice |
| Grapes |
| Low fat yoghurt |
| Fruit bread |
| Baked beans |
| Chocolate |
| **Foods with an Intermediate G.I. factor (G.I. 55-70)** |
| Basmati rice |
| Banana |
| Rolled oats |
| Soft drinks |
| Sweet corn |
| Pineapple |
| White sugar |
| **Foods with a high G.I. factor (G.I. > 70)** |
| Bread (white or whole meal) |
| Baked potato |
| Cornflakes |
| French Fries |

Recent studies indicate that high fibre and low GI foods not only help control diabetes, but also reduce the risk of diabetes. Reducing the diet glycaemic load by consuming low starch foods (low GI foods), increases insulin secretion to a significantly greater extent, than reducing glycaemic load by eating lesser carbohydrates. In Australia, the Glycaemic Index Foundation has been established. It certifies low GI foods, and allows a food manufacturer to use their symbol, so that it is easier for a consumer in choosing products. While giving certification, other nutritional criteria, such as calories, fat, saturated fats and/or salt are also considered.

## FATS

Your body needs fat to provide energy, and to help absorb fat soluble vitamins.

Vitamins A, D, E, and K are fat-soluble, meaning they can only be digested, absorbed, and transported in the body in conjunction with fats. Fats are also sources of essential fatty acids, an important dietary requirement.

Fats play a vital role in maintaining healthy skin and hair, insulating body organs against shock, maintaining the body temperature, and promoting healthy cell function.

Fats also serve as energy stores for the body, and contain about nine calories (kcal) per gram of fat. They are broken down in the body to release glycerol and free fatty acids. The glycerol can be converted to glucose by the liver, and thus used as a source of energy.

Fats also serve as a useful buffer against a host of diseases. When a particular substance, whether chemical or biotic – reaches unsafe levels in the bloodstream, the body can effectively dilute, or at least maintain the equilibrium of the offending substances, by storing it in new fat tissue. This helps to protect vital organs, until such time that the offending substances can be metabolized, and/ or removed from the body by means such as excretion, urination, accidental or intentional bloodletting, sebum excretion and hair growth. Consumption of certain fatty acids is important for the brain, and for the growth and development of infants.

Fats are most commonly made of a glycerol molecule – a three carbon molecule that acts as the backbone, to which a number of long chains of carbon acids, known as fatty acids, are attached. Typically three fatty acids are attached to each of the three carbon atoms of a single glycerol molecule, and therefore, fats are also called triglycerides. In case, if one fatty acid is attached, it is known as a monoglyceride, and if two fatty acids are attached, it is known as diglycerides.

The fatty acids which are attached to the carbon atom of glycerol, are of different lengths of the carbon chain. The carbon chain of fatty acid has a single bond, but at a certain position, it has a double bond. The double bond shows unsaturation, meaning there is scope for addition of a radical like the hydrogen ion. If, in the structure of the fatty acid, there is one double bond, the fatty acid is known as monounsaturated. When there are more double bonds, the fatty acid is known as polyunsaturated. In case, if there is no double bond in the fatty acid, then the fat is called saturated. The nomenclature of fatty acids is based on the length of the carbon chain, degree of unsaturation, and the position of the double bond in the carbon chain.

All vegetable oils contain all three types of acids (monounsaturated, polyunsaturated and saturated) in varying proportions. They are all in liquid form, but as they are hydrogenated, they are converted into saturated fat, and their form changes from liquid to solid. During hydrogenation (i.e. addition of hydrogen), if the addition of the hydrogen atom is on the same side of the carbon of the unsaturated fatty acid, the saturated fat is known to have *cis* form, but if it is not so, then the fat is known as trans fat. *Cis* fat results in a kink, or branching of fats, whereas the *trans* version forms a straight chain. It is believed that kinking or branching of fats, does not allow them to be stacked, one on top of the other, at the molecular level. As a result, they do not tend to solidify easily. On the other hand, *trans* fats are straight chains, meaning that they can be stacked easily. Therefore, they tend to solidify, and also resist metabolization.

The consumption of *trans* fats and saturated fats, increases the risk of coronary heart disease by raising the levels of LDL cholesterol (bad cholesterol), and lowering levels of HDL cholesterol (good cholesterol). Both these substances are metabolites of fat molecules. It is believed that bad cholesterol reacts with calcium ions and other materials, and forms an insoluble compound which gets deposited in the coronary artery of the heart. It forms blockages in the passages of blood circulation. As a result, the heart has to pump blood against the blockage, and has to exert more pressure leading to a heart attack. In view of these facts, health professionals recommend:

- keeping total fat intake between 20-35 per cent of calories
- avoiding dietary fats that increase cholesterol
- avoiding *trans* fats
- choosing monounsaturated and polyunsaturated fats from such sources as nuts, vegetable oils etc.

For the guidance of the reader, a chart of comparative dietary fats has been provided, so as to enable the reader to choose oils for consumption.

The role of fats in diets have always remained controversial. This can be seen from Table 9.2, which lists the evolving recommendations regarding fat consumption in dietary guidelines for Americans.

**Table 9.2:** Evolving Recommendations Regarding Fat Consumption in Dietary Guidelines for Americans (Courtesy: Professor Penny Kris-Etherton, USA)

| |
|---|
| 1980: Avoid too much **fat, saturated fat** and **cholesterol**. |
| 1990: Select a diet low in **fat, saturated fat** and **cholesterol**. |
| 2000: Select a diet low in **saturated fat, cholesterol** and moderate in **total fat** |
| 2005: Choose fats wisely: Limit intake of fats and oils high in **saturated** and/or **trans fat**. Get **mono** and **polyunsaturated fat** from fish, nuts, and vegetable oils. |

Recently, a very interesting cover story appeared in the February 2009 issue of *Food Technology* magazine published by the Institute of Food Technologists, USA (IFT). IFT is the apex association of all food technology-related professionals worldwide. The magazine is widely read internationally, and considered very authentic and prestigious. The article titled *'Rethinking Dietary Saturated Fat'* was written by Eric Westman, Associate Professor of Medicine, and Director of the Lifestyle Medicine Clinic at the Duke University School of Medicine, Durham, North Carolina.

The article says that the link between dietary fat and human disease is not conclusive. Medical policy makers, after raising the standards of evidence-based medicine, discovered that decisions based on observational evidence were not supported by subsequent randomized trials. Given this new evidence-based medicine standard, several groups reviewed the randomized controlled trials regarding dietary fats and cardiovascular diseases, and found that the evidence was not conclusive. An article in the *British Medical Journal* states that despite decades of efforts, and many thousands of people randomized, there is still only limited and inconclusive evidence of the effects of the modification of total, saturated, mono unsaturated, or polyunsaturated fats, on cardiovascular morbidity and mortality.

The author of the article finds carbohydrate linked diseases growing. Three parameters of cardio-metabolic risk – Low Density Lipoprotein (LDL), Triglyceride and High Density Lipoprotein (HDL) are measured, of which triglyceride and HDL improve with the lowering of carbohydrate intake. The author carried out a study to understand the effects of a low glycaemic, reduced calorie diet vs a low carbohydrate ketogenic diet (containing fat from cheese, whole eggs, etc.), and it was found, that the low carbohydrate ketogenic diet improved all other features of the metabolic syndrome, apart from LDL, triglycerides and HDL. Recently, a prominent researcher concluded – the overall evidence accumulated about diet, disease and health may be nearing a paradigm shift, in which prior observed facts remain, while beliefs about their accepted interpretation change. In other words, the consensus opinion is changing.

Unspent calories derived from food consumption, get converted into fat which is stored in various parts of the body. Fat Free Mass (FFM), also known as Lean Body Mass (LBM), is made up of structural and functional elements in the cells, body water, muscles, bones, minerals and other body organs such as the heart, liver and kidneys. It contains approximately 73 per cent water, 20 per cent protein, 6 per cent minerals and 1 per cent ash. The excessive accumulation of fat in the body weight, beyond the limitations of the skeletal and physical requirements results in obesity. Also, the modern way of life is stressful, and lacks even moderate exercising. As a result, incidences of several medical conditions have arisen. Obesity is a serious problem, and as a consequence, problems of cardiovascular diseases, diabetes and even low self-esteem are increasing at a rapid pace.

## PROTEINS

Proteins are the basic building blocks of life. Proteins serve two broad purposes in the human body, one for the formation or growth of the body and two, for carrying out physiological functions. Insulin, hemoglobin, myosin, etc., are functional proteins. Keratin and collagen are structural proteins.

There is a class of chemicals known as amino acids. They are nitrogen containing (amino group) acids, and there are about 20 such amino acids. Proteins are polymers of amino acids, and are therefore also commonly called polypeptides. The linkage between two amino acids is called peptide linkage. These 20 different amino acids can combine in thousands of different permutations and combinations, to give rise to hundreds of thousands of different protein structures. Proteins are known to fold into different patterns, based on their structure. Differences in patterns leads to the difference in the functionality of the protein. Hence, starting with only 20 basic amino acids, the body is able to produce thousands of different functional proteins in the body. As a matter of fact, we need thousands of different proteins for the functioning of our body.

Without proteins, metabolic activities will stop. Metabolic activities are required for energy. For metabolic activity, enzymes are required to act as catalysts. All enzymes are proteins. If metabolic activity stops, functioning of all the five basic human body systems namely circulation, digestion, nervous, renal and immune systems, get affected.

Apart from physiological functions, proteins are also required for the growth of the body. Growing children require more proteins in their diet, compared to adults.

When we eat foods, the protein content or polypeptide chains present in the food are broken down in the digestive tract, into the individual amino acids, which are then absorbed into our bodies. These amino acids are then recombined into different proteins as described earlier, specific to each individual person, in a process called protein synthesis. Synthesis of proteins in the body is a very complex process and proteins are synthesized as per the genetic code. The sequence and length of the amino acids which are responsible for a specific function of the protein, is guided by the code. The quality of dietary protein is expressed by its Protein Efficiency Ratio (PER). The weight gained per gram of protein in rats during feeding, is a measure of the PER. In case of proteins derived from animals such as meat, fish, etc., it is 4.0. In case of vegetable proteins such as groundnut, soya, pulses, etc., it is around 2.0. The efficiency could be improved by enriching vegetable proteins by the addition of two sulphur containing acids, namely lysine and methionine. These amino acids cannot be synthesized in the body, and hence they are known as essential amino acids.

## FIBRE

It is a nutrient which does not get absorbed in the digestive tract, and therefore does not release calories. Fibres are oligosaccharides and play an important role in promoting digestive health, by stimulating the growth of normal beneficial bacteria in the digestive tract. Fibres are therefore known as prebiotic. Fibres also help in absorption of certain beneficial nutrients, such as calcium, and restrict harmful nutrients. Due to better absorption of calcium, it promotes bone health. Fibres are known to reduce the cholesterol levels also. There are two types of fibres – soluble and insoluble, and they both function differently. Soluble fibres get dissolved in water just as sugar in water. Many fruits, vegetables and cereals contain both types of fibres. It is believed that soluble fibres play an important role in lowering cholesterol, whereas insoluble fibres help in improving gut health. Experts think that both the types of fibres are required in the diet. Vegetarians derive fibres from cereals, vegetables, fruits, etc., but meat and other animal product eaters need to supplement their diet with fibres.

## VITAMINS AND MINERALS

Vitamins and minerals are required in micro-quantities by the body, but they play a pivotal role in the proper functioning of body organs. There are two types of vitamins – water soluble and fat soluble. Vitamins A, D, E and K are fat soluble, whereas other vitamins namely the B group of vitamins and Vitamin C are water soluble.

Vitamin A is necessary for the development and protection of certain cells in the body. It is essential for the good health of eyes. Vitamin D plays an important part in the formation of bones and teeth. The deficiency of Vitamin D causes rickety legs in children. Vitamin E has a role in the reproductive function. It is also an antioxidant, and strengthens the electrolytes and prevents their fragmentation. Vitamin K is responsible for the clotting of blood, in case of surgery.

The Vitamin B group plays a role in the development of the body, appetite, nerves and skin. Vitamin B-12 is for the prevention of anaemia, which is widely prevalent among women in India. Vitamin C is an antioxidant, and it has many functions, such as helping in the healing of wounds, improving immunity, etc. It plays a role in the synthesis of steroid hormones in the body. Amongst the minerals – calcium, phosphorus, sodium, potassium, iron, sulphur, magnesium, iodine, chlorine, zinc and chromium are important for the functioning of the body.

Bones and teeth need calcium and 99 per cent of the total requirements of calcium is for maintaining their health. Along with calcium, bones and teeth also require phosphorus. Eighty per cent of the requirement of phosphorus is for bones and teeth, whereas the remaining 20 per cent is for the formation of biochemicals like DNA and ATP which are very essential for metabolic processes. We consume salt, i.e. sodium chloride. Sodium is an important constituent of the extra cellular fluids. It maintains blood pressure, and patients of high blood pressure are advised to reduce salt consumption. There are lots of processed foods which declare that they are low sodium and/or give sodium content per serving. In India, the salt sold is fortified with potassium iodate since both are required for the body. Potassium is an important constituent of cellular fluid. Iodine is a constituent of the secretion of the thyroid gland which is a hormone known as Thyroxin. Iron is required for the formation of hemoglobin. Seventy per cent of the iron in the body is in the haemoglobin, whereas the remaining is stored in the liver, spleen, bones and in other parts. In the absence of iron, the cells cannot take up oxygen, or eliminate carbon dioxide.

Nearly 50 per cent of the magnesium in the body is found in the bones, and the remaining 50 per cent in the cells. Magnesium is necessary for the activation of many enzymes. Sulphur is a constituent of protein. It is present in two amino acids, namely lysine and methionine. Chlorine is taken as a part of salt, and also functions in association with sodium. Chlorine is also a constituent of the digestive juices of the stomach.

Table 9.3 gives details of the nutritional value of typical Indian foods.

**Table 9.3:** Nutritional Values of Typical Indian Foods (Courtesy: Fatfreekitchen.com)

| *Food Indian Vegetable/ Curries* | *Portion (g)* | *Calories (Cal)* | *Carbohydrates (g)* | *Proteins (g)* | *Total Fat (g)* |
|---|---|---|---|---|---|
| Aloo-Baingan Mixed Vegetable | 100 | 103 | 32.3 | 1.3 | 4.7 |
| Aloo-Beans Mixed Vegetable | 100 | 134 | 34.3 | 2.4 | 8.7 |
| Aloo Curry | 100 | 105 | 14.4 | 1.2 | 5.0 |
| Baigan Ka Bharta | 100 | 70 | 5.7 | 1.2 | 4.7 |
| Bhindi (Okra) | 100 | 161 | 12.1 | 3.9 | 10.7 |
| Cabbage (Patta Gobhi) | 100 | 131 | 7.0 | 2.3 | 5.0 |
| Chhole (Chick Peas) | 100 | 74 | 3.3 | 4.3 | 4.1 |
| Curry, Kadhi (Besan Kadhi) | 100 | 100 | 15.0 | 2.9 | 5.1 |
| Gatte ki Subji | 148 | 275 | - | - | - |
| Methi Aloo | 100 | 121 | 16 | 2.2 | 5.4 |
| Mutter Paneer | 100 | 147 | 10.7 | 8.5 | 8.1 |
| Kaddu (Pumpkin, Kashiphal) | 100 | 67 | 6.7 | 1.6 | 3.8 |
| Rajmah (Kidney Beans) | 100 | 102 | 10.7 | 4.7 | 3.4 |
| Shahi Paneer | 95 | 263 | - | - | - |
| Simla Mirch Aloo | 100 | 93 | 12.8 | 1.5 | 3.4 |
| Stuffed Tomato | 100 | 85 | 11 | 2.1 | 3.4 |
| Torai (Ridge Gourd) | 100 | 65 | 4.0 | 1.2 | 4.7 |
| Vegetable Jalfrazi | 98 | 159 | - | - | - |
| Vegetable Kofta Curry | 100 | 147 | 13.3 | 2.6 | 9.1 |
| Vegetable Korma | 100 | 88 | 8.7 | 1.4 | 5.3 |

| *Food Indian Vegetable/ Curries* | *Portion (g)* | *Calories (Cal)* | *Carbohy-drates (g)* | *Proteins (g)* | *Total Fat (g)* |
|---|---|---|---|---|---|
| *Indian Dals* | | | | | |
| Arhar Dal | 100 | 53 | 8.0 | 2.8 | 1.2 |
| Chana Dal | 100 | 99 | 12.8 | 4.5 | 3.2 |
| Dal Makhani, Low Fat | 100 | 117 | 14.0 | 6.8 | 1.3 |
| Maah ki Dal | 146 | 92 | - | - | - |
| Moong Dal | 100 | 211 | 31.3 | 12.8 | 3.7 |
| Masoor Dal | 100 | 165 | 24.7 | 10.3 | 2.7 |
| Urad Dal | 100 | 107 | 14.0 | 6.0 | 3.0 |
| Sambhar | 100 | 5.0 | 2.6 | 15.0 | 1.8 |
| Dal Dhokli | 105 | 238 | - | - | - |
| *Indian Rice* | | | | | |
| Boiled Rice | 100 | 111 | 25.0 | 2.2 | 0.2 |
| Pulao | 100 | 119 | 190 | 3.2 | 3.4 |
| Khichadi | 100 | 215 | 33.0 | 4.3 | 7.4 |
| *Indian Milk Items* | | | | | |
| Milk (Buffalo) | 100 | 117 | 5.0 | 4.3 | 6.5 |
| Milk (Cow) | 100 | 67 | 4.4 | 3.2 | 4.1 |
| Curd (Cow's milk) | 100 | 60 | 3.0 | 3.1 | 4.0 |
| Butter milk | 100 | 15 | 0.5 | 0.6 | 1.1 |
| Skimmed milk | 100 | 29 | 4.6 | 2.5 | 0.1 |
| Paneer (Cow's milk) | 100 | 265 | 1.2 | 18.3 | 20.8 |
| Paneer (Buffalo's milk) | 100 | 292 | 7.9 | 13.4 | 23.0 |
| Khoya (Whole milk) | 100 | 421 | 20.5 | 20.0 | 25.9 |
| Khoya (Skimmed milk) | 100 | 206 | 25.7 | 22.3 | 1.6 |
| Cheese | 100 | 348 | 6.3 | 24.1 | 25.1 |
| Lassi | 100 | 69 | 3.2 | 5.7 | 0.5 |

| *Food Indian Vegetable/ Curries* | *Portion (g)* | *Calories (Cal)* | *Carbohy-drates (g)* | *Proteins (g)* | *Total Fat (g)* |
|---|---|---|---|---|---|
| *Indian Desserts/Sweets* | | | | | |
| Besan Laddu | 40 | 315 | -- | -- | -- |
| Carrot Halwa | 135 | 460 | -- | -- | -- |
| Coconut Barfi | 30 | 157 | -- | -- | -- |
| Kaju Rolls | 14 | 83 | -- | -- | -- |
| Kheer Rice | 150 | 345 | -- | -- | -- |
| Kulfi Malai | 75 | 210 | -- | -- | -- |
| Kulfi Mango | 70 | 147 | -- | -- | -- |
| Malpua | 40 | 342 | -- | -- | -- |
| Naan Khatai | 45 | 150 | -- | -- | -- |
| Rasgulla | 40 | 194 | -- | -- | -- |
| Sandesh | 7 | 30 | -- | -- | -- |
| Shrikhand | 105 | 465 | -- | -- | -- |
| Til Laddu | 20 | 55 | -- | -- | -- |
| *Miscellaneous Foods* | | | | | |
| Boondi Raita | 145 | 169 | -- | -- | -- |
| Coriander Chutney | 25 | 72 | -- | -- | -- |
| Coconut Chutney | 20 | 83 | -- | -- | -- |
| Dosa | 1 no | 145 | | | |
| Dosa Onion | 1 no | 157 | -- | -- | -- |
| Idli | 1 no | 69 | 15 | 1.2 | 0.2 |
| Pakoda Onion | 58 | 315 | -- | -- | -- |
| Pakoda Paneer | 125 | 376 | -- | -- | -- |
| Potato Tikki | 1 no | 60 | 3.4 | 0.2 | 5 |
| Rava Dosa with Chutney | 1 no | 97 | -- | -- | -- |
| Samosa | 1 no | 369 | 48.1 | 6.3 | 17.6 |

Presently, studies are going on in nutrigenomics. With the completion of the human genome project, and continuous study of individual genes, it is possible to establish a relationship between nutrition and genetic diseases. It may also be possible to correlate with dietary recommendations for different communities.

## INTRICATE RELATIONSHIP BETWEEN FOOD AND HEALTH

The more we learn about foods, the more we find that what we know is very little and have to learn a lot more. Since ages, people are aware of the relationship between food and health. Today, all over the world, practitioners of different medical therapies such as allopathy, ayurveda, homeopathy and naturopathy advise their patients to follow a certain food regime. Of course, all the systems do not prescribe the same regime, but there is no denying the relationship between food and health. In the past, many religious leaders recommended to their followers, not to consume certain foods. Even today, Muslims do not eat pig (pork) meat. Hindus do not consume cow meat (beef). Muslims do not eat *Jhatka* meat, and Hindus don't consume *halal*. Amongst vegetarians, Jains do not eat potatoes, onions, garlic and other root vegetables. All such recommendations must have a basis, and in all probability, this could be from epidemiological studies.

With the help of modern science, it is possible to identify toxic substances in a number of natural foods, which we consume. A number of legumes are found to contain naturally occurring toxic substances as part of their composition, in addition to aflatoxin which is produced by microbes when stored in fields. Even spices contain toxins, which are found to be carcinogenic, when tested on animals. As such, many of the food items are found to contain carcinogenic substances in their natural form, but we have been consuming such foods since generations. If one goes by current food laws, which are applied to ensure the safety of new food additives, such foods should not be permitted for consumption. Health authorities know about such products, but they cannot dare to rock the boat. They take a lenient view since such products have a long history of consumption, because they have been consumed for generations.

There are several food products which are derived from plants – such as cereals, fruits and vegetables, legumes, spices, nuts, etc. They contain bioactive chemicals, other than vitamins and minerals. These chemicals are called phytochemicals. There are many types of phytochemicals, but amongst them, antioxidants are the most important. Our body, while carrying out the metabolism of carbohydrates, fats and proteins, produces many free radicals of oxygen which damage the DNA, arteries, etc., in the body, leading to premature aging and deterioration in health. It is also known that environmental pollution, toxic chemicals and radiation enhance the production of these free radicals of oxygen. These cause diseases like cancer, increased risk of heart failure, etc. The presence of antioxidants gives protection by minimizing production of the free radicals of oxygen. There are various antioxidants such as carotenoids, lutein, flavonoids, anthocyanins, isoflavones, phenolic compounds in addition to certain vitamins and amino acids.

There are many compounds that are useful in preventing cancer, and are also anti inflammatory. Many compounds are found to be anti-microbial, and are effective even against pathogenic bacteria, and food born fungi. Scientists are also trying to determine the relationship between the composition of foods and satiety, food consumption and development of desire to consume more, etc. Religious and spiritual leaders believe that there is a relationship between composition of foods and personality attributes. Consumption of certain foods makes people more violent, lose control over anger, etc. Studies on the human genome project and of individual genes is in progress, and maybe we will have answers to some of the questions that we have today. But, in the meantime we should be cautious about consumption of foods on the basis of certain established facts.

Some people cannot digest milk. Such people are known as lactose intolerant. For the digestion of milk, an enzyme called lactase is required, and people having this problem are deficient in this enzyme.

When raw vegetables and fruits are stored after peeling and cutting for a long time, they get contaminated with microbes. Also, cooked foods when stored for a longer time than the usual time, during which they are supposed to be consumed, also get contaminated with microbes. The contamination with bacteria produces toxins leading to an outbreak of food poisoning. In India, such outbreaks happen many times in the summer season, after marriage parties.

Another important issue is of food allergies. In the United States, problems of food allergies affect as many as 5 per cent of the infants, less than three years of age and 3-4 per cent of adults. Allergy to food is an exaggerated immune response, triggered by a specific food. In the case of children, they are able to outgrow their allergy if they avoid the offending foods, when they are young. Our body has an immune system for defending itself against certain harmful substances, such as bacteria, viruses and toxins. In case of food allergy, the body mistakenly gives an immune response, causing hives, hoarse voice and wheezing. The symptoms develop in less than two hours. There could be many other symptoms such as abdominal pain, *diarrhoea*, difficulty in swallowing, itching in the mouth, throat, eyes, skin or any area, fainting, nausea, runny nose, patches of itch, scaly skin, peeling skin or blisters, swelling of eyelids, face, lips, tongue, shortness of breath, stomach cramps, vomiting, etc. Food allergies can trigger or worsen asthma, eczema, or other disorders. At times, complications can take place, which could be fatal.

The foods known to cause allergy are eggs, milk, peanuts, shellfish, soy, tree nuts, wheat, etc., in the case of children, and fish, peanuts, shellfish, tree nuts, etc., in the case of adults. Some fruits and vegetables are also known to cause allergies. It is not only the food that causes allergies, but also the genetic make up of an individual. Allergy practitioners have methods of finding out which foods cause problems for individuals. Anyone diagnosed with a food allergy is advised to carry an epinephrine injection and get trained in how to use it in an emergency. There was a person who was allergic to chickpea flour in India, but did not know that he was allergic to soy preparations. When he went to the United States, he consumed a soy product and the reaction was so severe that he passed away in minutes. It is prudent to study the ingredient list on the label, before consuming a new product.

Most people do not know of the food-drug interactions. After several years, the Indian Pharmacopeia Commission has published a National Formulary of India (NFI). The NFI explains what one should remember about food-drug interactions. Some of the points are listed below:

- There are ways to avoid placing the body at risk of an unwanted nutrient-drug interaction. An average consumer is usually ignorant about this. Precautions to be observed while taking medications, that will help avoid interactions.
- Read the prescription label on the container. If unable to understand something, or for more information, the patient may ask physician or pharmacist.
- Read directions, warnings and interactions precautions printed on all medication labels and package inserts. Even over-the-counter medications can cause problems.
- Take medication with a full glass of water.
- Do not stir medication into your food or take capsules apart (unless directed by your physician). This may change the way the drug works.
- Do not take vitamin pills at the same time you take medication-vitamins and minerals can interact with some drugs. Take vitamin and mineral supplements before, or after medicines.
- Do not mix medication with hot drinks, because the heat from the drink may destroy the effectiveness of the drug.
- Never take medication with alcoholic drinks.

- Be sure to tell your physician and pharmacist about all medications you are taking, both prescription and non-prescription.

The NFI in their Appendix 6D has provided three tables giving details of medications to be taken on an empty stomach, medications which should be taken with food and selected herbal or food products resulting in adverse effects.

# 10

# Food Laws

In 1954, a Bill was passed in parliament to make provisions for the prevention of adulteration of food. In 1955, formal rules were framed under the Act which are known as *The Prevention of Food Adulteration Rules 1955* generally called as the *PFA*. Under the Rules, the Central Government constituted a committee known as *The Central Committee of Food Standards (CCFS)*. Its role was to advise the central and state governments on matters arising out of the administration of the Act, and to carry out other functions assigned to it under the Act. The Rules gave definitions of terms such as *Adulterated* and *Misbranded Food*, etc., and indicated duties of the various government appointed officials like public analysts, food inspectors, health authorities, etc. It gave details of the power of courts to implead, or prosecute food manufacturers. It also described procedures for collection of samples, licensing, packaging and labelling of foods. It also provided details of the prescribed quality standards, use of food additives such as preservatives, colours, antioxidants, emulsifying and stabilizing agents, anti-caking agents, flavouring agents and related substances. Details were given on the restrictions on the use of pesticides, etc.

In 1955, the government under the *Essential Commodities Act, 1955* prepared an order known as *The Fruit Products Order 1955* also called *FPO*. The said order monitored the quality of products made out of fruits and vegetables, even though they would need to conform to PFA Rules. Similarly in 1998, the Ministry of Food and Consumer Affairs formulated an order – *The Edible Oils Packaging (Regulation) Order, 1998* under the Essential Commodities Act, 1955.

In 2006, parliament has enacted a law called *The Food Safety and Standards Act, 2006*. It is an Act to consolidate all the laws relating to food mentioned previously, and establishing the Food Safety and Standards Authority of India, for laying down science-based standards for articles of food, to regulate their manufacture, storage, distribution, sale and import, to ensure availability of safe and wholesome food for human consumption, and for matters connected therewith or incidental thereto. The Act came into force on 5 August 2011. Accordingly, a Food Authority was established with a Chairman and 22 members. Of the 22 members about one-third are women. There are several scientific panels which assist the Food Authority. They are:

1. Central Advisory Committee
2. Scientific panels which will have several sub-committees such as
   (*a*) Food additives, flavouring, processing aids and materials in contact with food
   (*b*) Pesticides and antibiotic residues
   (*c*) Genetically modified organisms and foods
   (*d*) Functional foods, nutraceuticals, dietetic products and other similar products
   (*e*) Biological hazards
   (*f*) Contaminants in the food chain
   (*g*) Labelling, and
   (*h*) Method of sampling and analysis
3. Scientific Committee

The Act also gives details of duties and functions of the Food Authority, General Principles of Food Safety, General Provisions for Articles of Food, Special Responsibilities for Food Safety,

Enforcement of the Act, Penalty and Punishment for Contravention, etc. Once this Act was enforced, the existing PFA and PFA rules, FPO, the Edible Oils Packaging (Regulation) Order, etc., ceased to operate.

There are no major changes related to quality standards, labelling rules, etc., but the new act has salient features regarding implementation. It will be enforced by state governments/union territories through the state commissioner for food safety, his officers and Panchayati Raj/municipal bodies. The Food Authority, and the state food safety authority responsible for enforcement, will appoint the commissioner of food safety and designated officers. They will also appoint food safety officers. The actual working will be as follows:

The food safety officer (FSO) will collect samples of food articles in four parts. Two of these parts will be sent to the designated officer (DO), one part to the laboratory, and if desired by the vendor, the remaining to an accredited laboratory.

1. Reports from both laboratories will go to the designated officer who will decide about further action, if the sample fails.
2. If the report indicates deliberate adulteration, attracting punishment of imprisonment, he will ask the commissioner of food safety to give sanction for prosecution in a special court. No civil court will have jurisdiction.
3. If two reports show variance, the designated officer will send one sample from his custody to a referral lab. If desired by the vendor, he may appeal to the designated officer to send the fourth sample to the referral lab.
4. In case the report indicates punishment with fine only, then the designated officer can fine petty business operators but in other cases, he will refer to the adjudication officer for suitable penalties.
5. If the food vendor is not satisfied with the decision of the adjudication officer, he can appeal to the tribunal.

The new Act also encourages visits of FSO's to manufacturer's facilities to inspect and give recommendations for improvements. On the whole, the new Act will reduce prosecution that is currently taking place and there will be quick disposal of cases. The new Act and rules are friendlier for genuine food processors. The old PFA and its rules in force for five decades, were many times deliberately misapplied, which was unreasonable, unfair and unjust. This resulted in too many cases in the courts, with very low rates of conviction. For example, if a manufacturer did not print a batch number on a package of food, even though it otherwise complied with all quality standards, he was still prosecuted and was charged with misbranding. The author faced this problem in a small town in Madhya Pradesh. We had printed the batch number on a label stuck on the bottle, but the number was not printed by mistake on the label stuck on the outer carton of the bottle. The label from the outer carton was removed and produced in the court as evidence. It took almost 17 years, and cost almost twenty-five thousand rupees (in the eighties, this was a significant amount) before the author was acquitted. In another case, in which a manufacturer and exporter of pickles/chutney was charged for misbranding for similar minor lapses, was arrested and denied bail for a month.

The charge of misbranding is serious when a manufacturer tries to mislead a consumer by persuasive and manipulative tall and/or false claims, about the use of the product. It is estimated that at least one million cases are pending in courts under the PFA rules, out of which many are pending for more than ten years. There may be many more cases of misbranding due to technical lapses, than for misleading claims.

Another important change is welcome in the new rules. This is the differentiation between adulteration of food (which is a willful act) and substandard food (where the food does not meet some quality parameters). In the earlier definition, adulterated food was defined when the article sold by a vendor was not of nature, substance or quality demanded by the purchaser and was to his prejudice, or was not of the nature, substance or quality which it purported or represented to be. In the new rules, the definition of adulteration is removed and instead, the definition of 'adulterant' is given, meaning any material which is or could be employed, for making the food unsafe, or sub-standard or mis-branded or containing extraneous matter. With this change, it is obvious that an article of food can be considered to be adulterated only when an adulterant is employed in the manufacture of the article. Many people knowingly and willfully employ adulterants, mainly with the aim of reducing the cost of the food, and improving its profits. These adulterants could be safe, or unsafe and may put the safety of the consumers at risk. Such cases must be severely punished, and possibly, with imprisonment. In the past, there were many cases where samples were declared adulterated, when they did not meet parameters such as moisture content. In such cases, no adulterant was used, but one or another the quality parameter did not meet the standards. For example, the food may have picked up moisture from the atmosphere due to poor packing.

Under the old rules, the food manufacturer or vendor had no option to get another sample analysed except through the court. The author knows of a particular instance, in which a small ice cream retail outlet ran into serious trouble due to an erroneous, and/or mischievous laboratory report. The owner of the retail outlet assumed that the sample of a well-known brand would never fail, but to his surprise, the sample was declared adulterated, due to the very low fat content. Obviously, the report was erroneous/ mischievous. The only option available to him was to get another portion of the sample tested in a referral laboratory through the court. Under the new rules, the designated officer gets two reports, and if there is a difference in the findings where, for example, if one of the reports fails the sample, he has an option to send the sample from his custody to the referral laboratory. In other words, he can decide about the further course of action on the basis of three reports. Earlier, on the basis of just one report, prosecution in the court had to be launched, and even health authorities had no option.

Most consumers think that there cannot be a discrepancy in the result of a report. They do not know that the accuracy of the results depends on factors such as.

1. Method of analysis
2. Reliability of instruments/reagents used in analysis
3. Skills and technical proficiency of the laboratory analyst, and
4. Honesty of the analyst

Sometimes, consumer organizations try to sensationalize laboratory findings particularly in the case of well-known brands, due to vested interests. The new Act envisages a large network of food labs to cope up with the increased work load. In such a case, it is imperative to ensure consistency and accuracy of the findings of all the laboratories. There could be discrepancies in laboratory findings, due to factors mentioned earlier. In the case of the larger multinational companies who are in the business of food manufacturing across different countries and have a large number of laboratories the world over – they ensure uniform testing by sending 'check samples' that have known parameters to their laboratories. Once the findings of different laboratories are obtained and compared, it becomes easier to identify shortcomings in the functioning of the laboratories. Our authorities will also have to follow such practices, since erroneous reports lead to confusion and wrongful punishment. In all fairness, such sensationalization should be done only after reconfirming the results with government accredited laboratories.

On these lines, there is also the need for an agency which can prepare 'check samples', and send them to various pathological laboratories which are not accredited. Many people must have come across discrepancies in the results of different laboratories, and as a result, patients have suffered dire consequences.

## TOUGH ISSUES YET TO BE ADDRESSED BY FOOD LAWS

After six decades of independence, there is not much of a change in the trade practices of primary foods sold in the market. A majority of the people living in urban and rural areas are poor. This class of people has little choice in buying quality foods. They have to procure primary foods from the ration shops, or small grocers. These are the outlets, where there are lots of quality issues, because the food items are not stored properly, and are sold in loose form. For this reason, our food laws permit foreign matter up to 1.0 per cent and also impurities of animal origin such as rodent excreta, rodent hair, etc., are permitted up to 0.1 per cent in agro commodities. It also permits damaged grain up to 5.0 per cent, weeviled grains from 5 per cent to 10 per cent, moisture content up to 14 per cent and toxic substances like aflatoxin up to 30 micrograms per kilo.

Under the new FSSA rules, limits have been provided for 149 insecticides and pesticides that are allowed to be present in articles of foods. Sometime back, there was a lot of hue and cry about insecticides and pesticides contamination in soft drink bottles. Author thinks it is a clear case of shooting the messenger instead of the real culprit. The problem of insecticides and pesticides is there because of the indiscreet use of these chemicals by farmers. Farmers use excessive quantities of these materials and there is no agency to monitor the use of these chemicals at a farm level. As a result, not only are most foods contaminated, but even the ground water is found to contain insecticides and pesticides in quantities higher than prescribed for drinking water. It is no wonder that mothers milk samples are reported to be contaminated with insecticides and pesticides. At present, the limit for insecticides such as DDT, endosuitan, hetachlorocyclohexane, malathion, etc., prescribed in carbonated drinks, is as low as 0.001 ppm (parts per million). On the other hand, limits for the same insecticides are set much higher for food items, which most people consume on a daily basis, such as fruits and vegetables, milk and milk products, meat, poultry and fish, food grains, etc. The limits for these insecticides in common food items are several thousand times higher than those prescribed for soft drinks. For example, the limit for DDT in carbonated drinks is 0.001 ppm whereas in eggs it is 0.5 ppm (500 times), meat poultry and fish is 7.0 ppm (7000 times), fruits and vegetables is 3.5 ppm (3500 times).

In case of another insecticide malathion, the limit for carbonated drinks is 0.001 ppm, whereas for the same insecticide, the limit for dried fruits is 8.0 ppm (8000 times), fruits is 4.0 ppm (4000 times) and vegetables 3.0 ppm (3000 times).

These examples give an insight into the problem areas and show that the problem of insecticides and pesticides is much more serious in case of primary foods, than things like soft drinks. In reality, food articles contain much more quantities of insecticides than what is permitted, but it is difficult to monitor the usage of these chemicals at the farm level. Also, it is very difficult to trace the source of primary foods, since they are sold in a loose form. Organic foods, i.e. food produced without the use of chemicals is the answer, but feeding a large population with organic foods is not feasible. The production of organic foods is reported to be expensive due to lower yield and higher cost of bio fertilizers and bio pesticides. In case if no pesticide is used, the farmer is taking a huge risk should there be pest infection to the crop. It would mean total loss of crop and he would be burdened with heavy financial losses. Many efforts are being made to find an economical solution to replace the use of pesticides but not with much success. In future when Genetically Modified crops are introduced, the problem of contamination of insecticides could be reduced due to the built in resistance to pests. But till then the focus has to be on farm practices.

Definition of *food* given in the Act includes packaged drinking water, but the act does not include water supplied by government agencies (like municipal corporations). Food processors are required to use water of drinking standards. Though the Water Pollution Prevention Act (1974) is in effect, the ground water in many places is contaminated with toxic materials from industrial effluents, and insecticides and pesticides indiscreetly used by farmers. There are several known diseases which are caused by the contamination of water by microbes, but there is much still to be known about the harm caused by contamination by chemicals.

These issues are not only important, but very serious, and they would require extraordinary efforts. Obviously, just food laws alone cannot solve these issues. The food sold by small street vendors in urban areas, and consumed by millions everyday, is not only prepared from poor quality ingredients, but also prepared and served in unhygienic conditions. One is also not sure about the personal hygiene and health of the food vendor. Such vendors are very large in numbers, and are scattered and unorganized. The Food Safety and Standards Act, 2006 does show the intention of bringing petty food vendors under licensing and registration under Section 31. Accordingly, all food vendors/operators including *kirana* stores, roadside vendors, caterers, etc., are covered. Food operators whose turnover is more than ₹ 1 lakh per month are required to obtain a license, and others are required to get registered. Those who fail to do so, may face punishment up to six months imprisonment and fine up to ₹ 5 lakh.

The FSSA is very much desirable, but in the present conditions, it is idealistic and ambitious. We have about twelve million *kirana* stores and millions of street vendors. For the first time, rules specify sanitary and hygiene requirements for street vendors by listing them in twenty-three points. They provide excellent guidelines, but it would be very difficult to ensure compliance This is because we have a huge number of vendors involved, and we have inadequate manpower and the organization to monitor, educate, train and persuade them to follow the requirements. The desired change would come only when consumers of food demand change. The demand from consumers will grow once they see the need and when their standard of living improves. At present, people who eat on the streets are very poor, and they decide to eat from a vendor on the basis of taste, price and quantity of serving. They are themselves not educated enough to appreciate the intangible and invisible benefits of having proper sanitary and hygienic conditions at the food vendor premises. Also, most such street vendors themselves come from a poor socio-economic background, where they have never seen proper sanitary and hygienic conditions, in order to implement them in their work. The need is therefore to create an awareness of the benefits of maintaining proper hygiene and sanitary conditions.

Only time will tell whether registration/licensing helps in improving the situation, or becomes an instrument for harassment of petty food vendors.

# 11

# Concluding Remarks

At the time when India got independence, agriculture contributed 70 per cent of GDP and accounted for 85 per cent of total employment. At that time, processed foods available in India were not many, as compared to these days. The government did not realize the importance of the food industry until the contribution of agriculture in the GDP steadily decreased. Today it is less than 20 per cent of the total GDP, though more than 60 per cent of the population still depends on agriculture. After the Ministry of Food Processing Industries (MOFPI) was set up in 1988, the processed food industry has started receiving due attention. Currently, the ministry has taken several steps to promote food processing by offering a number of incentives. The impact of these incentives will be felt in the future, but at present, the food industry accounts for only 1.0 per cent of total manufacturing activity. Only 25 per cent of the processed food industry is in the organized sector whereas 33 per cent is in the small scale and 42 per cent is in the unorganized sectors. In the international processed food trade, Indian processed foods account for only 1.5 per cent share of the market. It will always be difficult to export processed foods to the mainstream market of other countries by the small scale and unorganized sectors of the food industry. But, today they are exporting products mainly for Indian ethnic populations residing in the Middle East, the UK and the USA. It is difficult for food industries to export products under their own brand name in the mainstream market of other countries, but they can undertake manufacturing of processed foods for giant food companies. However, in order to do so, Indian manufacturers need to be cost effective. Multinational food companies could easily develop their manufacturing base in India for exporting goods to western countries, if they find it economically attractive.

In the coming years, Genetically Modified (GM) foods will find a place in the market. At present, there are lots of controversies about their safety and ecology concerns. GM foods are derived from genetically modified organisms. There are several genes in a living organism, and each gene is responsible for a specific biological function. Science is now so advanced, that it is possible to transfer a gene from one organism to another, so as to impart a specific change in the recipient organism. This technique is very precise. Earlier, such genetic changes were made by exposing an organism to radiation, or chemicals, but it could not produce a specific intended change. It would interest the reader to know that the drug insulin is produced by bacteria (a single cell organism) which never had the capability to do so earlier. It became possible after a human gene responsible for producing insulin was transferred to the bacteria by modern methods of genetic engineering. At present there are a number of foods in which a genetically modified version exists. Table 11.1 lists some of these foods. According to the information given in the table, in 2006 in the US, 93 per cent of the planted area of soybean, 93 per cent of cotton and 86 per cent of corn were genetically modified varieties. At present, the USA. accounts for 63 per cent, Argentina 21 per cent, Canada 6.0 per cent, Brazil 4.0 per cent and South Africa 1.0 per cent of the world's GM foods produced.

In India too, GM foods, namely Bt cotton and Bt brinjal are in the news at present. Both the products are of a multinational company, Monsanto. There is no doubt that once, more knowledge is gathered on genomes, safety evaluation methods, etc. GM foods will come to the market in a big way. At present, to produce more food, chemicals such as fertilizers and pesticides are used, though their excessive use has silently created unnoticed health problems. As demand for food increases, the government will have to choose the lesser evil between GM foods developed by a biological approach, or foods produced by the use of chemicals. Table 11.2 gives details of the research work in progress on GM food in various laboratories in India.

**Table 11.1:** Genetically Modified Foods
(Courtesy: Wikipedia)

| *Food* | *Properties of the Genetically Modified Variety* | *Modification* | *Per cent in US* | *Per cent in World* |
|---|---|---|---|---|
| Soybeans | Resistant to glyphosate or glufosinate herbicides | Herbicide resistant gene taken from bacteria inserted into soybean | 93% | 77% |
| Corn, field (Maize) | Resistant to glyphosate or glufosinate herbicides, Insect resistance via producing Bt proteins some previously used as pesticides in organic crop production. | New genes some from bacterium Bacillus thuringiensis added/transferred into plant genome | 86% | 26% |
| Cotton (cottonseed oil) | Pre resistant cotton | Bt crystal protein gene added/ transferred into plant genome | 93% | 49% |
| Hawaiian Papaya | Variety is resistant to the papaya ringspot virus | New gene added/ transferred into plant genome | 80% | |

| *Food* | *Properties of the Genetically Modified Variety* | *Modification* | *Per cent in US* | *Per cent in World* |
|---|---|---|---|---|
| Tomatoes | Variety in which the production of the enzyme polygalacturonase (PG) is suppressed, retarding fruit softening after harvesting. | A reverse copy (an antisense gene) of the gene responsible for the production of PG enzyme added into plant genome | Taken off the market due to commercial failure | Small quantities grown in China |
| Rice | Golden Rice. Genetically modified to contain beta carotene (source of Vitamin A) | Current version of Golden Rice under development contains genes from maize and a common soil microorganism. | Forecast to be on the market in 2013 | |
| Rapeseed (Canola) | Resistance to herbicides (glyphosate or glufosinate), high laurate canola | New genes added/transferred into plant genome | 93% | 21% |
| Sugarcane | Resistance to certain pesticides, high-sucrose content | New genes added/transferred into plant genome | | |
| Sugar beet | Resistance to glyphosate, glufosinate herbicides | New genes added/transferred into plant genome | 95% | 9% |
| Alfaalfa | Resistance to glyphosate, glufosinate herbicides | New genes added/transferred into plant genome | Planted in the US from 2005–2007 | |

**Table 11.2:** GM Foods Being Researched in India (Courtesy: Wikipedia)

| *Crop* | *Organization* |
|---|---|
| Brinjal | Mahyco, Mumbai<br>TNAU, Coimbatore<br>UAS, Dharwad<br>IVRI, Varanasi<br>Sungro Seeds Ltd, ND<br>IARI, ND |
| Cabbage | Nunhems India Pvt. Ltd.; Strip trials for bio-efficiency evaluation at Murthal, in Haryana, Bangalore |
| Cotton | Mahyco, Monsanto, Rasi, Nuziveedu, Ankur, JK Seeds, UAS-D |
| Cauliflower | Nunhems India Pvt. Ltd; Strip trials for bio-efficiency evaluation at Murthal, in Haryana, Bangalore<br>Sungro Seeds Ltd, ND; multilocation research trial on Bt Cauliflower hybrids |
| Groundnut | ICRISAT, Hyderabad |
| Maize | Monsanto, Mumbai |
| Chickpea | ICRISAT, Hyderabad |
| Mustard | UDSC, ND |
| Okra | Mahyco, Mumbai; Biosafety studies at Jalna, Maharashtra<br>Beejo Sheetal, Jalna |
| Pigeon pea | ICRISAT<br>Mahyco |
| Potato | CPRI, Shimla; Strip trials at CPRI, Modipuram<br>NIPGR, ND |
| Rice | Mahyco; trials at Nizamabad, Andhra Pradesh<br>TNAU, Coimbatore<br>Bayer Biosciences; contained field trials at Hyderabad |
| Sorghum | NRCS, Hyderabad |

| *Crop* | *Organization* |
|---|---|
| Tomato | National Research Centre for Plant Biotechnology, IARI, ND<br>Mahyco<br>NIPGR, ND<br>Avesthgen, Bangalore |
| Corn | Monsanto<br>Pioneer Overseas Corporation<br>Dow Agro Sciences |

## GM, BT AND HYBRIDS

*A **GENETICALLY*** modified (GM) crop is created when a foreign gene from a different species is introduced into a crop to enhance a certain quality. For example, a protein or a gene from say, a flower, can be introduced into a tomato.

*A **BT CROP*** is one in which the Bacillus Thuringiensis protein has been introduced, specifically to increase pest resistance. While a BT crop is a GM crop a GM crop is not always a BT crop. Both are transgenic.

*A **HYBRID CROP*** is created when two varieties of the same plant or crop are interbred to create a better crop. There is no genetic modification here.

To provide food security, output of agriculture should increase by at least 4.0 per cent. This can be achieved by reforms in agriculture to increase the yield of crops. At present, our yield of crops per acre is much less than many other countries. Development of the food industry will create employment in rural areas, and reduce wastage of foods. Reforms are also required in the marketing of farm produce to reduce intermediaries involved, who add on their margins. By reducing middlemen, farmers may realize better prices for their produce, and consumers will get foods at a reasonable price. But, it is easier said than done. It is not easy to eliminate the middlemen, because of a variety of issues, involving the demand and supply situation, logistics, transportation, financial aspects, government policy viz-à-viz imports and exports, etc. Once a proper supply chain is established, it would be easier to trace the source of quality issues, such as high pesticide residues.

These days, controversies about foods are not necessarily for genuine reasons. More often, they arise due to vested interests of a group of people. It is believed that the pesticide lobby is against introduction of GM food crops, since use of pesticides would be drastically reduced. The sugar lobby is known to be against non-nutritive sweeteners such as saccharine, aspartame, sucralose, etc. At times, controversies are also created against well-established branded products for competitive reasons. In all these types of controversies, politicians and decision makers should respect and trust the opinion of experts, and act in the best interests of the *aam aadmi*.

Unfortunately most decisions taken wittingly or unwittingly, have served the best interests of the *khas aadmi*, and Indian food laws are no exception. They will help making processed foods world class with details of nutritional information, and giving information on *trans* fats and warnings such as 'Not for phenylketonurics'. How many consumers can understand such information and benefit from it? Talking about *aam aadmi*, he does not even have access to safe-drinking water and adequate food. Even though the Prevention of Food Adulteration Act and its Rules (and now FSSA) have been in practice for more than five decades, deliberate adulteration of foods appears to be on the rise. Adulteration mostly takes place in items sold loose, and in primary foods. Ground spices are adulterated with sawdust and colours, milk with synthetic milk made out of caustic soda, urea and detergent. Also milk is adulterated with water of doubtful quality. Fruits are ripened with calcium carbide which is a carcinogenic substance, vegetables are coloured, sugar is mixed with chalk powder, honey with jaggery, etc. It is difficult to estimate the extent to which foods are adulterated, but one of the causes for adulteration are the high prices of foods.

Apart from adulteration of foods sold in loose form, there is a problem of counterfeit products of popular brands. It is not always possible to establish that the product under question is fake, because the counterfeit product manufacturer has cleverly matched those quality parameters that are generally measured in laboratories. In this situation, the manufacturer of branded products is helpless, and has to take the help of the police and other authorities for organizing a raid at the premises of the manufacturer of counterfeit products, while actual manufacturing is taking place, and catch him red handed. Knowing this weakness of a genuine manufacturer, there are many criminal minded people who are attracted to this activity. This problem also exists in the field of medicines, and other manufactured goods. Innovative technical solutions will be found, but it will increase the cost of the product.

The following issues are serious, since they affect a majority of the population:

- Foods containing high amounts of insecticides and pesticides
- Primary foods containing foreign matter
- Foods sold in unhygienic conditions in roadside eating places
- Foods adulterated with harmful materials, and
- Counterfeit products

The practice of drawing samples, sending them for analysis and then prosecuting the manufacturer, or vendor in the courts, based on laboratory reports, has not had the desired impact. In Maharashtra state alone, there are more than ten thousand cases pending in courts for more than ten years. Also as reported, the conviction rate is only 5 per cent. This could mean that genuine people are harassed and one is not sure if culprits are booked. They know how to escape from the net of the authorities.

Now that the new Food Safety and Standards Act, 2006 has come in force, one can expect some improvement. But, it is a challenging and uphill task. The members of the Central Advisory Committee have to play an important and pivotal role in improving the quality, and for ensuring that all citizens get foods that are safe to consume. Special efforts should be focused on the *aam aadmi,* since he spends as much as 70 per cent of his hard earned money for survival. The least he deserves is safe food, if not adequate quantities of food, or food of his choice.

At present the government has introduced a bill on food security for introducing it in the parliament. The intention of the bill is to ensure that people get adequate food at affordable prices. There are multiple views and debates on identifying that section of the population that is entitled to get food at subsidized rates. The Planning Commission of India has given new guidelines for covering people below the poverty line (BPL) which is defined as any person whose income is below thirty-two rupees a day in urban areas and twenty six rupees a day in rural areas. A person is expected to take care of *roti, kapda* and *makaan,* if he or she is earning above the limit prescribed. It is assumed that education and healthcare will be provided free by the government. It has been clarified by the authorities that for eligibility, and entitlement of benefits this limit will not be used. As such, there is a huge population of poor and vulnerable people just above the poverty line, and also the middle class. At least 80 per cent of the people deserve benefits under the food security act. Many people are intrigued with the idea of having the food security act, since more than 50 per cent of the population is engaged in food production activities, i.e. agriculture. In any case, the current system of PDS, and centralized procurement and distribution is far from satisfactory. This can be observed from the data given in the following Table 11.3 published in the *Indian Express* dated 7 January, 2011 in an article '*A Costly Morality*' written by Shri Surjit Bhalla.

The first two rows show the difference in terms of tonnes of food that was siphoned out of the system. This food went from PDS shops to the market for resale to the poor, at market prices. The subsidy value of this tax payers loss, and gain for the middlemen works out at about ₹ 30,000 crore. This is a huge amount. There are many government schemes which provide subsidy, but the subsidy on food is in a way special. First and foremost, the amount of subsidy involved is huge, and it is almost always on a perpetual basis. Also, there is a strong emotional appeal for expenditure, since everyone will support the cause for feeding a hungry person.

**Table 11.3:** Public Distribution System (PDS) Govt. of India versus National Sample Survey (Courtesy: RBI Handbook of Statistics, Ministry of Finance, Budget Statements, Different Years)

| | *UNIT* | *2004-2005* | *2009-2010* |
|---|---|---|---|
| Distribution of food via PDS Ration Shops | Mn Tonnes | 41.5 | 48.9 |
| PDS Food Received by the population, NSS | Mn Tonnes | 13.2 | 25.3 |
| % leakage of Food via PDS ration shops | | 68.2% | 48.3% |
| Food Subsidy – Ministry of Finance | ₹ crores | 24479 | 59621 |
| Food Subsidy according to NSS | ₹ crores | 8474 | 38875 |
| PDS corruption estimate | ₹ crores | 16005 | 20746 |

**Notes**: PDS subsidy has been calculated by using NSS PDS price and NSS market price differential and multiplying it by NSS PDS consumption.

There is another angle to providing food security. The famous old Chinese proverb says, "Don't give a fish to a hungry person – it will feed him for a day. Teach him how to fish and he will feed himself for life". Experts believe that for a permanent solution for food security, agricultural output per hectare needs to be increased, which is currently very low, when compared to other countries. They also believe that the income levels of people should rise so that they can afford to pay for food. It is possible to achieve both the goals, if the huge amounts on subsidies are reduced and the money is spent instead on schemes for improving the yields of agricultural output and lowering costs of production. Also, this will result in sparing agricultural land for industrial purposes thus leading to more employment and increase in income levels. Of course, for all these measures, political will is required.

Being an optimist, I believe that '*woh subah kabhi to aayegi*'. After all '*kiske roke ruka hai savera?*'

# ANNEXURE

## INTERNATIONAL NUMBERING SYSTEM (INS) FOR FOOD ADDITIVES

The following list is only for identifying the food additive and their synonyms as published by the Codex on 23.11.2005 Codex. For the latest updates, JECFA/Codex website may be referred to (www.codexalimentarius.net, www.codexalimentarius.net/web/jecfa.jsp)

### List Sorted by INS Number

| *Sl. No.* | *INS Number* | *Food Additive Name* | *Technical Functions* |
|---|---|---|---|
| *1* | *2* | *3* | *4* |
| 1. | 100 | Curcumins | Colour |
| 2. | 100(i) | Curcumin | Colour |
| 3. | 100(ii) | Turmeric | Colour |
| 4. | 101 | Riboflavins | Colour |
| 5. | 101(i) | Riboflavin | Colour |
| 6. | 101(ii) | Riboflavin 5′-phosphate, sodium | Colour |
| 7. | 102 | Tartrazine | Colour |
| 8. | 103 | Alkanet | Colour |
| 9. | 104 | Quinoline yellow | Colour |
| 10. | 107 | Yellow 2G | Colour |
| 11. | 110 | Sunset yellow FCF | Colour |
| 12. | 120 | Carmines | Colour |
| 13. | 121 | Citrus red 2 | Colour |
| 14. | 122 | Azorubine/Carmoisine | Colour |
| 15. | 123 | Amaranth | Colour |
| 16. | 124 | Ponceau 4R | Colour |
| 17. | 125 | Ponceau SX | Colour |
| 18. | 127 | Erythrosine | Colour |
| 19. | 128 | Red 2G | Colour |

| *Sl. No.* | *INS Number* | *Food Additive Name* | *Technical Functions* |
|---|---|---|---|
| *1* | 2 | 3 | 4 |
| 20. | 129 | Allurared AC/Fast Red E | Colour |
| 21. | 130 | Manascorubin | Colour |
| 22. | 131 | Patent blue V | Colour |
| 23. | 132 | Indigotine | Colour |
| 24. | 133 | Brilliant blue FCF | Colour |
| 25. | 140 | Chlorophyll | Colour |
| 26. | 141 | Copper chlorophylls | Colour |
| 27. | 141(i) | Chlorophyll copper complex, | Colour |
| 28. | 141(ii) | Chlorophyll copper complex, sodium and potassium Salts | Colour |
| 29. | 142 | Green S | Colour |
| 30. | 143 | Fast green FCF | Colour |
| 31. | 150a | Caramel I – plain | Colour |
| 32. | 150b | Caramel II – caustic sulphite process | Colour |
| 33. | 150c | Caramel III – ammonia process | Colour |
| 34. | 150d | Caramel IV – ammonia sulphite Process | Colour |
| 35. | 151 | Brilliant black PN | Colour |
| 36. | 152 | Carbon black (hydrocarbon) | Colour |
| 37. | 153 | Vegetable carbon | Colour |
| 38. | 154 | Brown FK | Colour |
| 39. | 155 | Brown HT | Colour |
| 40. | 160a | Carotenes | Colour |
| 41. | 160a(i) | Beta-carotene (synthetic) | Colour |
| 42. | 160a(ii) | Natural extracts | Colour |
| 43. | 160b | Annatto extracts | Colour |
| 44. | 160c | Paprika Oleoresins | Colour |

| *Sl. No.* | *INS Number* | *Food Additive Name* | *Technical Functions* |
|---|---|---|---|
| *1* | 2 | 3 | 4 |
| 45. | 160d | Lycopene | Colour |
| 46. | 160e | Beta-apo-carotental | Colour |
| 47. | 160f | Beta-apo-8′-carotenic acid, methyl or ethyl ester | Colour |
| 48. | 161a | Flavoxanthin | Colour |
| 49. | 161b | Lutein | Colour |
| 50. | 161c | Krytoxanthin | Colour |
| 51. | 161d | Rubixanthin | Colour |
| 52. | 161e | Violoxanthin | Colour |
| 53. | 161f | Rhodoxanthin | Colour |
| 54. | 161g | Canthaxanthin | Colour |
| 55. | 162 | Beet red | Colour |
| 56. | 163 | Anthocyanins | Colour |
| 57. | 163(i) | Anthocyanins | Colour |
| 58. | 163(ii) | Grape skin extract | Colour |
| 59. | 163(iii) | Blackcurrant extract | Colour |
| 60. | 164 | Gardenia yellow | Colour |
| 61. | 166 | Sandalwood | Colour |
| 62. | 170 | Calcium carbonates | Surface colourant, anticaking agent, stabilizer |
| 63. | 170(i) | Calcium carbonate | Anticaking agent |
| 64. | 170(ii) | Calcium hydrogen carbonate | Anticaking agent |
| 65. | 171 | Titanium dioxide | Colour |
| 66. | 172 | Iron oxides | Colour |
| 67. | 172(i) | Iron oxide, black | Colour |
| 68. | 172(ii) | Iron oxide, red | Colour |
| 69. | 172(iii) | Iron oxide, yellow | Colour |
| 70. | 173 | Aluminium | Colour |
| 71. | 174 | Silver | Colour |
| 72. | 175 | Gold | Colour |

| *Sl. No.* | *INS Number* | *Food Additive Name* | *Technical Functions* |
|---|---|---|---|
| *1* | *2* | *3* | *4* |
| 73. | 180 | Lithol rubine BK | Colour |
| 74. | 181 | Tannins, food grade | Colour, emulsifier, stabilizer, thickener |
| 75. | 182 | Orchil | Colour |
| 76. | 200 | Sorbic acid | Preservative |
| 77. | 201 | Sodium sorbate | Preservative |
| 78. | 202 | Potassium sorbate | Preservative |
| 79. | 203 | Calcium sorbate | Preservative |
| 80. | 209 | Heptyl p-hydroxybenzoate | Preservative |
| 81. | 210 | Benzoic acid | Preservative |
| 82. | 211 | Sodium benzoate | Preservative |
| 83. | 212 | Potassium benzoate | Preservative |
| 84. | 213 | Calcium benzoate | Preservative |
| 85. | 214 | Ethyl p-hydroxybenzoate | Preservative |
| 86. | 215 | Sodium ethyl p-hydroxybenzoate | Preservative |
| 87. | 216 | Propyl p-hydroxybenzoate | Preservative |
| 88. | 217 | Sodium propyl p-hydroxybenzoate | Preservative |
| 89. | 218 | Methyl p-hydroxybenzoate | Preservative |
| 90. | 219 | Sodium methyl p-hydroxybenzoate | Preservative |
| 91. | 220 | Sulphur dioxide | Preservative, antioxidant |
| 92. | 221 | Sodium sulphite | Preservative, antioxidant |
| 93. | 222 | Sodium hydrogen sulphite | Preservative, antioxidant |
| 94. | 223 | Sodium metabisulphite | Preservative, bleaching agent, antioxidant |

| *Sl. No.* | *INS Number* | *Food Additive Name* | *Technical Functions* |
|---|---|---|---|
| *1* | *2* | *3* | *4* |
| 95. | 224 | Potassium metabisulphite | Preservative, antioxidant |
| 96. | 225 | Potassium sulphite | Preservative, antioxidant |
| 97. | 226 | Calcium sulphite | Preservative, antioxidant |
| 98. | 227 | Calcium hydrogen sulphite | Preservative, antioxidant |
| 99. | 228 | Potassium bisulphate | Preservative, antioxidant |
| 100. | 230 | Diphenyl | Preservative |
| 101. | 231 | Ortho-phenylphenol | Preservative |
| 102. | 232 | Sodium o-phenylphenol | Preservative |
| 103. | 233 | Thiabendazole | Preservative |
| 104. | 234 | Nisin | Preservative |
| 105. | 235 | Pimaricin (natamycin) | Preservative |
| 106. | 236 | Formic acid | Preservative |
| 107. | 237 | Sodium formate | Preservative |
| 108. | 238 | Calcium formate | Preservative |
| 109. | 239 | Hexamethylene tetramine | Preservative |
| 110. | 240 | Formaldehyde | Preservative |
| 111. | 241 | Gum guaicum | Preservative |
| 112. | 242 | Dimethyl dicarbonate | Preservative |
| 113. | 249 | Potassium nitrite | Preservative, colour fixative |
| 114. | 250 | Sodium nitrite | Preservative, colour fixative |
| 115. | 251 | Sodium nitrate | Preservative, colour fixative |
| 116. | 252 | Potassium nitrate | Preservative, colour fixative |
| 117. | 260 | Acetic acid, glacial | Preservative, acidity regulator |

| *Sl. No.* | *INS Number* | *Food Additive Name* | *Technical Functions* |
|---|---|---|---|
| *1* | *2* | *3* | *4* |
| 118. | 261 | Potassium acetates | Preservative, acidity regulator |
| 119. | 261(i) | Potassium acetate | Preservative, acidity regulator |
| 120. | 261(ii) | Potassium diacetate | Preservative, acidity regulator |
| 121. | 262 | Sodium acetates | Preservative, acidity regulator, sequestrant |
| 122. | 262(i) | Sodium acetate | Preservative, acidity regulator, sequestrant |
| 123. | 262(ii) | Sodium diacetate | Preservative, acidity regulator, sequestrant |
| 124. | 263 | Calcium acetate | Preservative, stabilizer, acidity regulator |
| 125. | 264 | Ammonium acetate | Acidity regulator |
| 126. | 265 | Dehydroacetic acid | Preservative |
| 127. | 266 | Sodium dehydroacetate | Preservative |
| 128. | 270 | Lactic acid (L-, D-and Dl-) | Acidity regulator |
| 129. | 280 | Propionic acid | Preservative |
| 130. | 281 | Sodium propionate | Preservative |
| 131. | 282 | Calcium propionate | Preservative |
| 132. | 283 | Potassium propionate | Preservative |
| 133. | 290 | Carbon dioxide | Carbonating agent, packing agent |
| 134. | 296 | Malic acid (DL-L-) | Acidity regulator, flavouring agent |
| 135. | 297 | Fumaric acid | Acidity regulator |
| 136. | 300 | Ascorbic acid (L) | Antioxidant |
| 137. | 301 | Sodium ascorbate | Antioxidant |
| 138. | 302 | Calcium ascorbate | Antioxidant |
| 139. | 303 | Potassium ascorbate | Antioxidant |
| 140. | 304 | Ascorbyl palmitate | Antioxidant |

| *Sl. No.* | *INS Number* | *Food Additive Name* | *Technical Functions* |
|---|---|---|---|
| *1* | *2* | *3* | *4* |
| 141. | 305 | Ascorbyl stearate | Antioxidant |
| 142. | 306 | Mixed tocopherols | Antioxidant |
| 143. | 307 | Alpha-tocopherol | Antioxidant |
| 144. | 308 | Synthetic gamma-tocopherol | Antioxidant |
| 145. | 309 | Synthetic delta-tocopherol | Antioxidant |
| 146. | 310 | Propyl gallate | Antioxidant |
| 147. | 311 | Octyl gallate | Antioxidant |
| 148. | 312 | Dodecyl gallate | Antioxidant |
| 149. | 313 | Ethyl gallate | Antioxidant |
| 150. | 314 | Guaiac resin | Antioxidant |
| 151. | 315 | Isoascorbic acid | Antioxidant |
| 152. | 316 | Sodium isoascorbate | Antioxidant |
| 153. | 317 | Potassium isoascorbate | Antioxidant |
| 154. | 318 | Calcium isoascrobate | Antioxidant |
| 155. | 319 | Tertiary butylhydroquinone | Antioxidant |
| 156. | 320 | Butylated hydroxyanisole | Antioxidant |
| 157. | 321 | Butylated hydroxytoluene | Antioxidant |
| 158. | 322 | Lecithins | Antioxidant, emulsifier |
| 159. | 323 | Anoxomer | Antioxidant |
| 160. | 324 | Ethoxyquin | Antioxidant |
| 161. | 325 | Sodium lactate | Antioxidant, synergist, humectant, bulking agent |
| 162. | 326 | Potassium lactate | Antioxidant, synergist, acidity regulator |
| 163. | 327 | Calcium lactate | Acidity regulator, flour treatment agent |

| *Sl. No.* | *INS Number* | *Food Additive Name* | *Technical Functions* |
|---|---|---|---|
| *1* | 2 | *3* | *4* |
| 164. | 328 | Ammonium lactate | Acidity regulator, flour treatment agent |
| 165. | 329 | Magnesium lactate (D-, L-) | Acidity regulator, flour treatment agent |
| 166. | 330 | Citric acid | Acidity regulator, synergist for Sequestrant |
| 167. | 331 | Sodium citrates | Acidity regulator, sequestrant emulsifier stabilizer |
| 168. | 331(i) | Sodium dihydrogen citrate | Acidity regulator, sequestrant emulsifer, stabilizer |
| 169. | 331(ii) | Disodium monohydrogen citrate | Acidity regulator, stabilizer, sequestrant, emulsifier |
| 170. | 331(iii) | Trisodium citrate | Acidity regulator, sequestrant, emulsifier, stabilizer |
| 171. | 332 | Potassium citrates | Acidity regulator, sequestrant, stabilizer |
| 172. | 332(i) | Potassium dihydrogen citrate | Acidity regulator, sequestrant, stabilizer |
| 173. | 332(ii) | Tripotassium citrate | Acidity regulator, sequestrant, stabilizer |
| 174. | 333 | calcium citrates | Acidity regulator, firming agent, sequestrant |
| 175. | 334 | Tartaric acid [L(+)-] | Acidity regulator, sequestrant, antioxidant synergist |
| 176. | 335 | Sodium tartrates | Stabilizer, sequestrant |
| 177. | 335(i) | Monosodium tartrate | Stabilizer, sequestrant |
| 178. | 335(ii) | Disodium tartrate | Stabilizer, sequestrant |
| 179. | 336 | Potassium tartrate | Stabilizer, sequestrant |

| *Sl. No.* | *INS Number* | *Food Additive Name* | *Technical Functions* |
|---|---|---|---|
| *1* | *2* | *3* | *4* |
| 180. | 336(i) | Monopotassium tartrate | Stabilizer, sequestrant |
| 181. | 336(ii) | Dipotassium tartrate | Stabilizer, sequestrant |
| 182. | 337 | Potassium sodium tartrate | Stabilizer, sequestrant |
| 183. | 338 | Orthophosphoric acid | Acidity regulator, antioxidan synergist |
| 184. | 339 | Sodium phosphates | Acidity regulator, texturizer, sequestrant, stabilizer |
| 185. | 339(i) | Monosodium orthophosphate | Acidity regulator, texturizer, sequestrant, stabilizer, emulsifier, water retention agent |
| 186. | 339(ii) | Disodium orthophosphate | Acidity regulator, texturizer, sequestrant, stabilizer |
| 187. | 339(iii) | Trisodium orthophosphate | Sequestrant, stabilizer, Emulsifier, water retention agent, acidity regulator, texturizer |
| 188. | 340 | Potassium Phosphates | Acidity regulator, texturizer, sequestrant, stabilizer, emulsifier, water retention agent |
| 189. | 340(i) | Monopotassium orthophosphate | Acidity regulator, texturizer, sequestrant, stabilizer emulsifier, water retention agent |
| 190. | 340(ii) | Dipotassium orthophosphate | Acidity regulator, texturizer, sequestrant, stabilizer, emulsifier, water retention agent |
| 191. | 340(iii) | Tripotassium orthophosphate | Acidity regulator, texturizer, sequestrant, stabilizer, emulsifier, water retention agent |

| *Sl. No.* | *INS Number* | *Food Additive Name* | *Technical Functions* |
|---|---|---|---|
| *1* | *2* | *3* | *4* |
| 192. | 341 | Calcium phosphates | Acidity regulator, texturizer, water retention agent, flour treatment agent, raising agent, firming agent, anticaking agent |
| 193. | 341(i) | Monocalcium orthophosphate | Acidity regulator, texturizer, water retention agent, flour treatment agent, firming agent, anticaking agent |
| 194. | 341(ii) | Dicalcium orthophosphate | Acidity regulator, texturizer, flour treatment agent, raising agent, firming agent, anticaking agent |
| 195. | 341(iii) | Tricalcium orthophosphate | Acidity regulator, texturizer, water retention agent, flour treatment agent, firming agent, anticaking agent |
| 196. | 342 | Ammonium phosphates | Acidity regulator, flour treatment agent |
| 197. | 342(i) | Monoamonium orthophosphate | Acidity regulator, flour treatment agent |
| 198. | 342(ii) | Diammonium orthophosphate | Acidity regulator, flour treatment agent |
| 199. | 343 | Magnesium phosphates | Acidity regulator, anticaking agent |
| 200. | 343(i) | Monomagnesium orthophosphate | Acidity regulator, anticaking agent |
| 201. | 343(ii) | Dimagnesium orthophosphate | Acidity regluator, anticaking agent |

| *Sl. No.* | *INS Number* | *Food Additive Name* | *Technical Functions* |
|---|---|---|---|
| *1* | *2* | *3* | *4* |
| 202. | 343(iii) | Trimagnesium orthophosphate | Acidity regulator, anticaking agent |
| 203. | 344 | Lecithin citrate | Preservative |
| 204. | 345 | Magnesium citrate | Acidity regulator |
| 205. | 349 | Ammonium malate | Acidity regulator |
| 206. | 350 | Sodium malates | Acidity regulator, humectant |
| 207. | 350(i) | Sodium hydrogen malate | Acidity regulator, humectant |
| 208. | 350(ii) | Sodium malate | Acidity regulator, humectant |
| 209. | 351 | Potassium malates. | Acidity regulator |
| 210. | 351(i) | Potassium hydrogen malate | Acidity regulator |
| 211. | 351(ii) | Potassium malate | Acidity regulator |
| 212. | 352 | Calcium malates | Acidity regulator |
| 213. | 352(i) | Calcium hydrogen malate | Acidity regulator |
| 214. | 352(ii) | Calcium malate | Acidity regulator |
| 215. | 353 | Metatartaric acid | Acidity regulator |
| 216. | 354 | Calcium tartrate | Acidity regulator |
| 217. | 355 | Adipic acid | Acidity regulator |
| 218. | 356 | Sodium adipates | Acidity regulator |
| 219. | 357 | Potassium adipates | Acidity regulator |
| 220. | 359 | Ammonium adipates | Acidity regulator |
| 221. | 363 | Succinic acid | Acidity regulator |
| 222. | 364(i) | Monosodium succinate | Acidity regulator, flavour enhancer |
| 223. | 364(ii) | Disodium succinate | Acidity regulator, flavour enhancer |
| 224. | 365 | Sodium fumarates | Acidity regulator |
| 225. | 366 | Potassium fumarates | Acidity regulator |
| 226. | 367 | Calcium fumarates | Acidity regulator |

| *Sl. No.* | *INS Number* | *Food Additive Name* | *Technical Functions* |
|---|---|---|---|
| *1* | *2* | *3* | *4* |
| 227. | 368 | Ammonium fumarates | Acidity regulator |
| 228. | 370 | 1, 4-Heptonolactone | Acidity regulator, sequestrant |
| 229. | 375 | Nicotinic acid | Colour retention agent |
| 230. | 380 | Ammonium citrates | Acidity regulator |
| 231. | 381 | Ferric ammonium citrate | Anticaking agent |
| 232. | 383 | Calcium glycerophosphate | Thickener, gelling agent, stabilizer |
| 233. | 384 | Isopropyl citrates | Antioxidant, preservative, sequestrant |
| 234. | 385 | Calcium disodium ethylene- diamine-tetra-acetate | Antioxidant, preservative, sequestrant |
| 235. | 386 | Disodium ethylene-diamine-tetra-acetate | Antioxidant, preservative, sequestrant |
| 236. | 387 | Oxy stearin | Antioxidant, sequestrant |
| 237. | 388 | Thiodipropionic acid | Antioxidant |
| 238. | 389 | Dilauryl thiodipropionate | Antioxidant |
| 239. | 390 | Distearyl thiodipropionate | Antioxidant |
| 240. | 391 | Phytic acid | Antioxidant |
| 241. | 399 | Calcium lactobionate | Stabilizer |
| 242. | 400 | Alginic acid | Thickener, stabilizer |
| 243. | 401 | Sodium alginate | Thickener, stabilizer, gelling agent |
| 244. | 402 | Potassium alginate | Thickener, stabilizer |
| 245. | 403 | Ammonium alginate | Thickener, stabilizer |
| 246. | 404 | Calcium alginate | Thickener, stabilizer, gelling agent, antifoaming agent |

| *Sl. No.* | *INS Number* | *Food Additive Name* | *Technical Functions* |
|---|---|---|---|
| *1* | *2* | *3* | *4* |
| 247. | 405 | Propylene glycol alginate | Thickener, emulsifier |
| 248. | 406 | Agar | Thickener, gelling agent, stabilizer |
| 249. | 407 | Carrageenan and its Na, K, NH4salts (includes furcellaran) | Thickener, gelling agent, stabilizer |
| 250. | 407a | Processed Euchema Seaweed (PES) | Thickener, stabilizer |
| 251. | 408 | Bakers yeast glycan | Thickener, gelling agent, stabilizer |
| 252. | 409 | Arabinogalactan | Thickener, gelling agent, stabilizer |
| 253. | 410 | Carob bean gum | Thickener, stabilizer |
| 254. | 411 | Oat gum | Thickener, stabilizer |
| 255. | 412 | Guar gum | Thickener, stabilizer, emulsifier |
| 256. | 413 | Tragacanth gum | Thickener, stabilizer, emulsifier |
| 257. | 414 | Gum arabic (acacia gum) | Thickener, stabilizer |
| 258. | 415 | Xanthan gum | Thickener, stabilizer, emulsifier, foaming agent |
| 259. | 416 | Karaya gum | Thickener, stabilizer |
| 260. | 417 | Tara gum | Thickener, stabilizer |
| 261. | 418 | Gellan gum | Thickener, stabilizer, gelling agent |
| 262. | 419 | Gum ghatti | Thickener, stabilizer, emulsifier |
| 263. | 420 | Sorbitol and sorbitol syrup | Sweetener, humectant, sequestrant, texturizer, Emulsifier |
| 264. | 421 | Mannitol | Sweetener, anticaking agent |

| *Sl. No.* | *INS Number* | *Food Additive Name* | *Technical Functions* |
|---|---|---|---|
| *1* | *2* | *3* | *4* |
| 265. | 242 | Glycerol | Humectant, bodying agent |
| 266. | 244 | Curd lan | Thickener, stabilizer |
| 267. | 225 | Konjac flour | Thickener |
| 268. | 429 | Peptones | Emulsifier |
| 269. | 430 | Polyoxyethylene (8) stearate | Emulsifier |
| 270. | 431 | Polyoxyethylene (40) stearate | Emulsifier |
| 271. | 432 | Polyoxyethylene (20) sorbitan Monolaurate | Emulsifier, dispersing agent |
| 272. | 433 | Polyoxyethylene (20) sorbitan Monoleate | Emulsifier, dispersing agent |
| 273. | 434 | Polyoxyethylene (20) sorbitan Monopalmitate | Emulsifier, dispersing agent |
| 274. | 435 | Polyoxyethylene (20) sorbitan Monostearate | Emulsifier, dispersing agent |
| 275. | 436 | Polyoxyethylene (20) sorbitan Tristearate | Emulsifier, dispersing agent |
| 276. | 440 | Pectins | Thickener, emulsifier, stabilizer, gelling agent |
| 277. | 441 | Superglycerinated hydrogenated rapeseed oil | Emulsifier |
| 278. | 442 | Ammonium salts of phosphatidic Acid | Emulsifier |
| 279. | 443 | Brominated vegetable oil | Emulsifier, stabilizer |
| 280. | 444 | Sucrose acetate isobutyrate | Emulsifier, stabilizer |
| 281. | 445 | Glycerol esters of wood resin | Emulsifier, stabilizer |
| 282. | 446 | Succistearin | Emulsifier |

| *Sl. No.* | *INS Number* | *Food Additive Name* | *Technical Functions* |
|---|---|---|---|
| *1* | 2 | 3 | 4 |
| 283. | 450 | Diphosphates | Acidity regulator, texturizer, sequestrant, stabilizer, emulsifier, water retention agent |
| 284. | 450(i) | Disodium diphosphate | Acidity regulator, texturizer, sequestrant, stabilizer, emulsifier, water retention agent |
| 285. | 450(ii) | Trisodium diphosphate | Acidity regulator, texturizer, sequestrant, stabilizer, emulsifier, water retention agent |
| 286. | 450(iii) | Tetrasodium diphosphate | Acidity regulator, texturizer, sequestrant, stabilizer, emulsifier, water retention agent |
| 287. | 450(iv) | Dipotassium diphosphate | Acidity regulator, texturizer, sequestrant, stabilizer, emulsifier, water retention agent |
| 288. | 450(v) | Tetrapotassium diphosphate | Emulsifier, stabilizer, acidity regulator, raising agent sequestrant, water retention agent |
| 289 | 450(vi) | Dicalcium diphosphate | Acidity regulator, texturizer, sequestrant stabilizer, emulsifier, water retention agent |
| 290. | 450(vii) | Calcium dihydrogen diphosphate | Emulsifier, raising agent, stabilizer, sequestrant, acidity, regulator, water retention agent |
| 291. | 450 | Dimagnesium diphosphate | Acidity regulator, texturizer, sequestrant, stabilizer, emulsifier, water retention Agent |

| *Sl. No.* | *INS Number* | *Food Additive Name* | *Technical Functions* |
|---|---|---|---|
| *1* | *2* | *3* | *4* |
| 292. | 451 | Triphosphates | Acidity regulator, texturizer, sequestrant, stabilizer, emulsifier, water retention agent |
| 293. | 451(i) | Pentasodium | Sequestrant, acidity regulator texturizer |
| 294. | 451(ii) | Pentapotassium triphosphate | Sequestrant, acidity regulator, texturizer |
| 295. | 452 | Polyphosphates | Sequestrant, acidity regulator, texturizer |
| 296. | 452(i) | Sodium polyphosphate | Acidity regulator, texturizer, sequestrant stabilizer, emulsifier, water retention agent |
| 297. | 452(ii) | Potassium polyphosphate | Acidity regulator, texturizer, sequestrant stabilizer, emulsifier, water retention agent |
| 298 | 452(iii) | Sodium calcium polyphosphate | Acidity regulator, texturizer, sequestrant stabilizer, emulsifier, water retention agent |
| 299. | 452(iv) | Calcium polyphosphates | Emulsifier, stabilizer, acidity regulator, raising agent, Sequestrant, water retention agent |
| 300. | 452(v) | Ammonium polyphosphates | Emulsifier, stabilizer, acidity regulator, raising agent, sequestrant, water retention agent |
| 301. | 458 | Gamma cyclodextrin | Stabilizer, binder |
| 302. | 459 | Beta-cyclodextrin | Stabilizer, binder |
| 303. | 460 | Cellulose | Emulsifier, dispersing agent, anticaking agent, texturizer |

| *Sl. No.* | *INS Number* | *Food Additive Name* | *Technical Functions* |
|---|---|---|---|
| *1* | *2* | *3* | *4* |
| 304. | 460(i) | Microcystalline cellulose | Emulsifier, dispersing agent, anticaking agent |
| 305. | 460(ii) | Powdered cellulose | Emulsifier dispersing agent, anticaking agent |
| 306. | 461 | Methyl cellulose | Thickener, emulsifier, stabilizer |
| 307. | 462 | Ethyl cellulose | Binder, filler |
| 308. | 463 | Hydroxypropyl cellulose | Thickener, emulsifier, stabilizer |
| 309. | 464 | Hydroxypropyl methyl cellulose | Thickener, emulsifier, stabilizer |
| 310. | 465 | Methyl ethyl cellulose | Thickener antifoaming agent, emulsifier, stabilizer |
| 311. | 466 | Sodium carboxymethyl cellulose | Thickener, emulsifier, Stabilizer |
| 312. | 467 | Ethyl hydroxyethyl cellulose | Thickener, emulsifier, Stabilizer |
| 313. | 468 | Croscaramellose | Stabilizer, binder |
| 314. | 469 | Sodium carboxymethyl cellulose, enzymatically hydrolysed | Thickener, stabilizer |
| 315. | 470 | Salts of fatty acids (with base Al, Ca, Na, Mg, K, and NH4) | Emulsifier, stabilizer, anticaking agent |
| 316. | 471 | Mono- and di-glycerides of fatty acids | Emulsifier, stabilizer |
| 317. | 472a | Acetic and fatty acid esters of glycerol | Emulsifier, stabilizer sequestrant |
| 318. | 472b | Lactic and fatty acid esters of glycerol | Emulsifier, stabilizer, sequestrant |
| 319. | 472c | Citric and fatty acid esters of glycerol | Emulsifier, stabilizer, sequestrant |

| *Sl. No.* | *INS Number* | *Food Additive Name* | *Technical Functions* |
|---|---|---|---|
| *1* | *2* | *3* | *4* |
| 320. | 472d | Tartaric acid esters of mono and diglycerides of fatty acids | Emulsifier, stabilizer, sequestrant |
| 321. | 472e | Diacetyltartric and fatty acid ester of glycerol | Emulsifier, stabilizer, sequestrant |
| 322. | 472f | Mixed tartaric, acetic and fatty acid esters of glycerol | Emulsifier, stabilizers, sequestrant |
| 323. | 472g | Succinylated monoglycerides | Emulsifier, stabilizer, sequestrant |
| 324. | 473 | Sucrose esters of fatty acids | Emulsifier, stabilizer, sequestrant |
| 325. | 474 | Sucroglycerides | Emulsifier, stabilizer, sequestrant |
| 326. | 475 | Polyglycerol esters of fatty acid | Emulsifier, stabilizer, sequestrant |
| 327. | 476 | Polyglycerol esters of interesterified ricinoleic acid | Emulsifier, stabilizer, sequestrant |
| 328. | 477 | Propylene glycol esters of fatty Acids | Emulsifier, stabilizer, sequestrant |
| 329. | 478 | Lactylated fatty acid esters of glycerol and propylene glycol | Emulsifier, stabilizer, sequestrant |
| 330. | 479. | Thermally oxidized soya bean oil with mono- and di-glycerides of fatty acids | Emulsifier, stabilizer, Sequestrant |
| 331. | 480 | Dioctyl sodium sulphosuccinate | Emulsifier, wetting agent |
| 332. | 481 | Sodium lactylate | Emulsifier, stabilizer |
| 333. | 481(i) | Sodium stearoyl lactylates | Emulsifier, stabilizer |
| 334. | 481(ii) | Sodium oleyl lactylate | Emulsifier, stabilizer |
| 335. | 482 | Calcium lactylates | Emulsifier, stabilizer |
| 336. | 482(i) | Calcium stearoyl lactylate | Emulsifier, stabilizer |

| *Sl. No.* | *INS Number* | *Food Additive Name* | *Technical Functions* |
|---|---|---|---|
| *1* | *2* | *3* | *4* |
| 337. | 482(ii) | Calcium oleyl lactylates | Emulsifier, stabilizer |
| 338. | 483 | Stearyl tartrate | Flour treatment agent |
| 339. | 484 | Stearyl citrate | Emulsifier, sequestrant |
| 340. | 485 | Sodium stearoyl fumarate | Emulsifier |
| 341. | 486 | Calcium stearoyl fumarate | Emulsifier |
| 342. | 487 | Sodium laurylsulphate | Emulsifier |
| 343. | 488 | Ethoxylated mono- and di-glycerides | Emulsifier |
| 344. | 489 | Methyl glucoside-coconut oil ester | Emulsifier |
| 345. | 491 | Sorbitan monostearate | Emulsifier |
| 346. | 492 | Sorbitan tristearate | Emulsifier |
| 347. | 493 | Sorbitan monolaurate | Emulsifier |
| 348. | 494 | Sorbitan monooleate | Emulsifier |
| 349. | 495 | Sorbitan monopalmitate | Emulsifier |
| 350. | 496 | Sorbitan trioleate | Stabilizer, emulsifier |
| 351. | 500 | Sodium carbonates | Acidity regulator, raising agent, anticaking agent |
| 352. | 500(i) | Sodium carbonate | Acidity regluator, raising agent, anticaking agent |
| 353. | 500(ii) | Sodium hydrogen carbonate | Acidity regulator, raising agent, anticaking agent |
| 354. | 500(iii) | Sodium sesquicarbonate | Acidity regulator, raising agent, anticaking agent |
| 355. | 501 | Potassium carbonates | Acidity regulator, stabilizer |
| 356. | 501(i) | Potassium carbonate | Acidity regulator, stabilizer |

| *Sl. No.* | *INS Number* | *Food Additive Name* | *Technical Functions* |
|---|---|---|---|
| *1* | *2* | *3* | *4* |
| 357. | 501(ii) | Potassium hydrogen carbonate | Acidity regulator, stabilizer |
| 358. | 503 | Ammonium carbonates | Acidity regulator, raising agent |
| 359. | 503(i) | Ammonium carbonate | Acidity regulator, raising agent |
| 360. | 503(ii) | Ammonium hydrogen carbonate | Acidity regulator, raising agent |
| 361. | 504 | Magnesium carbonates | Acidity regulator, anticaking agent, colour retention agent |
| 362. | 504(i) | Magnesium carbonate | Acidity regulator, anticaking agent, colour retention agent |
| 263. | 504(ii) | Magnesium hydrogen carbonate | Acidity regulator, anticaking agent, colour retention agent |
| 364. | 505 | Ferrous carbonate | Acidity regulator |
| 365. | 507 | Hydrochloric acid | Acidity regulator acid |
| 366. | 508 | Potassium chloride | Gelling agent |
| 367. | 509 | Calcium chloride | Firming agent |
| 368. | 510 | Ammonium chloride | Flour treatment agent |
| 369. | 511 | Magnesium chloride | Firming agent |
| 370. | 512 | Stannous chloride | Antioxidant, colour retention agent |
| 371. | 513 | Sulphuric acid | Acidity regulator |
| 372. | 514 | Sodium sulphates | Acidity regulator |
| 373 | 515 | Potassium sulphates | Acidity regulator |
| 374. | 516 | Calcium Sulphate | Dough conditioner, Sequestrant, firming agent |
| 375. | 517 | Ammonium sulphate | Flour treatment agent, stabilizer |
| 376. | 518 | Magnesium sulphate | Firming agent |

| *Sl. No.* | *INS Number* | *Food Additive Name* | *Technical Functions* |
|---|---|---|---|
| *1* | *2* | *3* | *4* |
| 377. | 519 | Cupric sulphate | Dolour fixative, preservative |
| 378. | 520 | Aluminium sulphate | Firming agent |
| 379. | 521 | Aluminium sodium Sulphate | Firming agent |
| 380. | 522 | Aluminium potassium Sulphate | Acidity regulator, stabilizer |
| 381. | 523 | Aluminium ammonium Sulphate | Stabilizer, firming agent |
| 382. | 524 | Sodium hydroxide | Acidity regulator |
| 383. | 525 | Potassium hydroxide | Acidity regulator |
| 384. | 526 | Calcium hydroxide | Acidity regulator, firming agent |
| 385. | 527 | Ammonium hydroxide | Acidity regulator |
| 386. | 528 | Magnesium hydroxide | Acidity regulator, colour retention agent |
| 387. | 529 | Calcium oxide | Acidity regulator, colour retention agent |
| 388. | 530 | Magnesium oxide | Anticaking agent |
| 389. | 535 | Sodium ferrocyanide | Anticaking agent |
| 390. | 536 | Potassium ferrocyanide | Anticaking agent |
| 391. | 537 | Ferrous hexacyanomanganate | Anticaking agent |
| 392. | 538 | Calcium ferrocyanide | Anticaking agent |
| 393. | 539 | Sodium thiosulphate | Antioxidant, sequestrant |
| 394. | 541 | Sodium aluminium phosphate | Acidity regulator, emulsifier |
| 395. | 541(i) | Sodium aluminium phosphate-acidic | Acidity regulator, emulsifier |
| 396. | 541(ii) | Sodium aluminium phosphate-basic | Acidity regulator, emulsifier |
| 397. | 542 | Bone phosphate (essentially calcium phosphate, tribasic) | Emulsifier, anticaking agent, water retention agent |

| *Sl. No.* | *INS Number* | *Food Additive Name* | *Technical Functions* |
|---|---|---|---|
| *1* | *2* | *3* | *4* |
| 398. | 550 | Sodium silicates | Anticaking agent |
| 399. | 550(i) | Sodium silicate | Anticaking agent |
| 400. | 550(ii) | Sodium metasilicate | Anticaking agent |
| 401. | 551 | Silicon dioxide, amorphous | Anticaking agent |
| 402. | 552 | Calcium silicate | Anticaking agent |
| 403. | 553 | Magnesium silicates | Anticaking agent, dusting powder |
| 404. | 553(i) | Magnesium silicate | Anticaking agent, dusting powder |
| 405. | 553(ii) | Magnesium trisilicate | Anticaking agent, dusting powder |
| 406. | 553(iii) | Talc | Anticaking agent, dusting powder |
| 407. | 554 | Sodium aluminosilicate | Anticaking agent |
| 408. | 555 | Potassium aluminium silicate | Anticaking agent |
| 409. | 556 | Calcium aluminium silicate | Anticaking agent |
| 410. | 557 | Zinc silicate | Anticaking agent |
| 411. | 558 | Bentonite | Anticaking agent |
| 412. | 559 | Aluminium silicate | Anticaking agent |
| 413. | 560 | Potassium silicate | Anticaking agent |
| 414. | 570 | Fatty acids | Foam stabilizer, glazing agent, antifoaming agent |
| 415. | 574 | Gluconic acid (D-) | Acidity regulator, raising agent |
| 416. | 575 | Glucono delta-lactone | Acidity regulator, raising agent |
| 417. | 576 | Sodium gluconate | Sequestrant |
| 418. | 577 | Potassium gluconate | Sequestrant |
| 419. | 578 | Calcium gluconate | Acidity regluator, firming agent |

| *Sl. No.* | *INS Number* | *Food Additive Name* | *Technical Functions* |
|---|---|---|---|
| *1* | *2* | *3* | *4* |
| 420. | 579 | Ferrous gluconate | Colour retention agent |
| 421. | 580 | Magnesium gluconate | Acidity regulator, firming agent |
| 422. | 585 | Ferrous lactate | Colour retention agent |
| 423. | 586 | 4-Hexylresorcinol | Colour retention agent, antioxidant |
| 424. | 620 | Glutamic acid (L (+)-) | Flavour enhancer |
| 425. | 621 | Monosodium glutamate | Flavour enhancer |
| 426. | 622 | Monopotassium glutamate | Flavour enhancer |
| 427. | 623 | Calcium glutamate | Flavour enhancer |
| 428. | 624 | Monoammonium glutamate | Flavour enhancer |
| 429. | 625 | Magnesium glutamate | Flavour enhancer |
| 430. | 626 | Guanylic acid | Flavour enhancer |
| 431. | 627 | Disodium 5′-guanylate | Flavour enhancer |
| 432. | 628 | Dipotassium 5′-guanylate | Flavour enhancer |
| 433. | 629 | Calcium 5′-guanylate | Flavour enhancer |
| 434. | 630 | Inosinic acid | Flavour enhancer |
| 435. | 631 | Disodium 5′-inosinate | Flavour enhancer |
| 436. | 632 | Potassium inosate | Flavour enhancer |
| 437. | 633 | Calcium 5′-inosinate | Flavour enhancer |
| 438. | 634 | Calcium 5′-ribonucleotides | Flavour enhancer |
| 439. | 635 | Disodium 5′-ribonucleotides | Flavour enhancer |
| 440. | 636 | Maltol | Flavour enhancer |
| 441. | 637 | Ethyl maltol | Flavour enhancer |
| 442. | 638 | Sodium L-Aspartate | Flavour enhancer |
| 443. | 639 | DL-Alanine | Flavour enhancer |
| 444. | 640 | Glycine | Flavour enhancer |

| *Sl. No.* | *INS Number* | *Food Additive Name* | *Technical Functions* |
|---|---|---|---|
| *1* | *2* | *3* | *4* |
| 445. | 641 | L-Leucine | Flavour enhancer |
| 446. | 642 | Lysin hydrochloride | Flavour enhancer |
| 447. | 900a | Polydimethylsiloxane | Antifoaming agent, anticaking agent, emulsifier |
| 448. | 900b | Methylphenylpolysiloxane | Antifoaming agent |
| 449. | 901 | Beeswax, white and yellow | Glazing agent, release agent |
| 450. | 902 | Candeilla Wax | Glazing agent |
| 451. | 903 | Carnaubawax | Glazing agent |
| 452. | 904 | Shellac | Glazing agent |
| 453. | 905a | Mineral oil, food grade | Glazing agent, release agent sealing agent |
| 454. | 905b | Petrolatum Petroleumielly | Glazing agent, release agent, sealing agent |
| 455. | 905c | Petroleum wax | Glazing agent, release agent, sealing agent |
| 456. | 905c(i) | Microcrystallinewax | Glazing agent |
| 457. | 905c(ii) | Paraffin wax | Glazing agent |
| 458. | 906 | Benzoin gum | Glazing agent |
| 459. | 907 | Hydrogenated poly-1 decene | Glazing agent |
| 460. | 908 | Rice bran wax | Glazing agent |
| 461. | 909 | Spermaceti wax | Glazing agent |
| 462. | 910 | Wax esters | Glazing agent |
| 463. | 911 | Methyl esters of fatty acids | Glazing agent |
| 464. | 913 | Lanolin | Glazing agent |
| 465. | 915 | Glycerol-, methyl-, or penta-erithrytol esters of colophane | Glazing agent |
| 466. | 916 | Calcium iodate | Flour treatment agent |
| 467. | 917 | Potassium iodate | Flour treatment agent |

| *Sl. No.* | *INS Number* | *Food Additive Name* | *Technical Functions* |
|---|---|---|---|
| *1* | *2* | *3* | *4* |
| 468. | 918 | Nitrogen oxide | Flour treatment agent |
| 469. | 919 | Nitrosyl chloride | Flour treatment agent |
| 470. | 920 | L-Cysteine and its hydrochlorides-sodium and potassium salts | Flour treatment agent |
| 471. | 921 | L-Cysteine and its hydrochlorides-sodium and potassium salts | Flour treatment agent |
| 472. | 922 | Potassium persulphate | Flour treatment agent |
| 473. | 923 | Ammonium persulphate | Flour treatment agent |
| 474. | 924a | Potassium bromate | Flour treatment agent |
| 475. | 924b | Calcium bromate | Flour treatment agent |
| 476. | 925 | Chlorine | Flour treatment agent |
| 477. | 926 | Chlorine dioxide | Flour treatment agent |
| 478. | 927a | Azodicarbonamide | Flour treatment agent |
| 479. | 927b | Carbamide (urea) | Flour treatment agent |
| 480. | 928 | Benzoyl peroxide | Flour treatment agent, Preservative |
| 481. | 929 | Acetone peroxide | Flour treatment agent |
| 482. | 930 | Calcium peroxide | Flour treatment agent |
| 483. | 938 | Argon | Packing gas |
| 484. | 939 | Helium | Packing gas |
| 485. | 940 | Dichlorodifluoro-methane | Propellant, liquid freezant |
| 486. | 941 | Nitrogen | Packing gas, freezant |
| 487. | 942 | Nitrous oxide | Propellant |
| 488. | 943a | Butane | Propellant |
| 489. | 943b | Isobutane | Propellant |
| 490. | 944 | Propane | Propellant |
| 491. | 945 | Chloropentafluo-roethane | Propellant |
| 492. | 946 | Octafluorocyclobutane | Propellant |

| *Sl. No.* | *INS Number* | *Food Additive Name* | *Technical Functions* |
|---|---|---|---|
| *1* | *2* | *3* | *4* |
| 493. | 948 | Oxygen | Packing gas |
| 494. | 950 | Acesulfame potassium | Sweetener, flavour enhancer |
| 495. | 951 | Aspartame | Sweetener, flavour enhancer |
| 496. | 952 | Cyclamic acid (and Na, K, Ca salts) | Sweetener |
| 497. | 953 | Isomalt (isomaltitol) | Sweetener, anticaking agent, bulking agent, glazing agent |
| 498. | 954 | Saccharin (and Na, K, Ca salts) | Sweetener |
| 499. | 955 | Sucralose (trichloro-galactosucrose) | Sweetener |
| 500. | 856 | Alitame | Sweetener |
| 501. | 957 | Thaumatin | Sweetener, flavour enhancer |
| 502. | 958 | Glycyrrhizin | Sweetener, flavour enhancer |
| 503. | 959 | Neohesperidine dihydrochalcone | Sweetener |
| 504. | 960 | Stevioside | Sweetener |
| 505. | 964 | Polyglycitol syrup | Sweetener |
| 506. | 965 | Maltitol and matitol Syrup | Sweetener, stabilizer, emulsifier |
| 507. | 966 | Lactitol | Sweetener, texturizer |
| 508. | 967 | Xylitol | Sweetener, humectant, stabilizer, emulsifier, thickener |
| 509. | 968 | Erythritol | Sweetener, flavour enhancer, humectant |
| 510. | 999 | Qulillaia extracts | Foaming agent |
| 511. | 1000 | Cholic acid | Emulsifier |
| 512. | 1001 | Choline salts and esters | Emulsifier |
| 513. | 1001(i) | Choline acentate | Emulsifier |

| *Sl. No.* | *INS Number* | *Food Additive Name* | *Technical Functions* |
|---|---|---|---|
| *1* | *2* | *3* | *4* |
| 514. | 1001(ii) | Choline carbonate | Emulsifier |
| 515. | 1001(iii) | Choline chloride | Emulsifier |
| 516. | 1001(iv) | Choline citrate | Emulsifier |
| 517. | 1001(v) | Choline tartrate | Emulsifier |
| 518. | 1001(vi) | Choline lactate | Emulsifier |
| 519. | 1100 | Amylases | Flour treatment agent |
| 520. | 1101 | Proteases | Flour treatment agent, stabilizer, tenderizer, flavour enhancer |
| 521. | 1101(i) | Protease | Flour treatment agent, stabilizer, tenderizer, flavour enhancer |
| 522. | 1101(ii) | Papain | Flour treatment agent, stabilizer, tenderizer, flavour enhancer |
| 523. | 1101(iii) | Bromelain | Flour treatment agent, stabilizer, tenderizer, flavour enhancer |
| 524. | 1101(iv) | Ficin | Flour treatment agent, stabilizer, tenderizer, flavour enhancer |
| 525. | 1102 | Glucose oxidase | Antioxidant |
| 526. | 1103 | Invertases | Stabilizer |
| 527. | 1104 | Lipases | Flavour enhancer |
| 528. | 1105 | Lysozyme | Preservative |
| 529. | 1200 | Polydextroses A and N | Bulking agent, stabilizer, thickener, humectant texturizer |
| 530. | 1201 | Polyvinylpyrrolidone | Bodying agent, stabilizer, clarifying agent, dispersing agent |
| 531. | 1202 | Polyvinylpoly-pyrrolidone | Colour stabilizer, colloidal, stabilizer |
| 532. | 1503 | Castor oil | Release agent |

| *Sl. No.* | *INS Number* | *Food Additive Name* | *Technical Functions* |
|---|---|---|---|
| *1* | *2* | *3* | *4* |
| 533. | 1505 | Triethyl citrate | Foam stabilizer |
| 534. | 1518 | Triacetin | Humectant |
| 535. | 1520 | Propylene glycol | Humectant, wetting agent, dispersing agent |
| 536. | 1521 | Polyethylene glycol | Antifoaming agent |
| *Supplementary List – Modified Starches* | | | |
| 537. | 1400 | Dextrins, roasted starch white and yellow | Stabilizer, thickener, binder |
| 538. | 1401 | Acid-treated starch | Stabilizer, thickener, binder |
| 539. | 1402 | Alkaline treated starch | Stabilizer, thickener, binder |
| 540. | 1403 | Bleached starch | Stabilizer, thickener, binder |
| 541. | 1404 | Oxidised starch | Stabilizer, thickener, binder |
| 542. | 1405 | Starches, enzyme-treated | Thickener |
| 543. | 1410 | Monostarch phosphate | Stabilizer, thickener, binder |
| 544. | 1411 | Distarch glycerol | Stabilizer, thickener, binder |
| 545. | 1412 | Distarch phosphate esterified with sodium trimetaphosphate; | Stabilizer, thickener, binder |
| 546. | 1413 | Phosphated distarch phosphate | Stabilizer, thickener, binder |
| 547. | 1414 | Acetylated distarch phosphate | Emulsifier, thickener, binder |
| 548. | 1420 | Starch acetate esterified with Acetic anhydride | Stabilizer, thickener |
| 549. | 1421 | Starch acetate esterified with vinyl acetate | Stabilizer, thickener |
| 550. | 1422 | Acetylated distarch adipate | Stabilizer, thickener, binder, emulsifier |

| *Sl. No.* | *INS Number* | *Food Additive Name* | *Technical Functions* |
|---|---|---|---|
| *1* | *2* | *3* | *4* |
| 551. | 1423 | Acetylated distarch glycord | Stabilizer, thickener |
| 552. | 1440 | Hydroxypropyl starch | Stabilizer, thickener, binder, emulsifier |
| 553. | 1442 | Hydroxypropyl distarch phosphate | Stabilizer, thickener |
| 554. | 1443 | Hydroxypropyl distarch | Stabilizer, thickener |
| 555. | 1450 | Starch sodium octenyl succinate | Stabilizer, thickener, binder |

# CHAPTER 1

**Photo 1.** Collaborative efforts on field

**Photo 2.** Garnished food

## CHAPTER 2

**Photo 3.** Mechanized farming in large fields

**Photo 4.** Farming in deserts with drip irrigation and controlled sunlight

**Photo 5.** Tea production by terrace farming

**Photo 6.** Silos – Proper way to store grains

# CHAPTER 3

**Photo 7.** Tray dryer

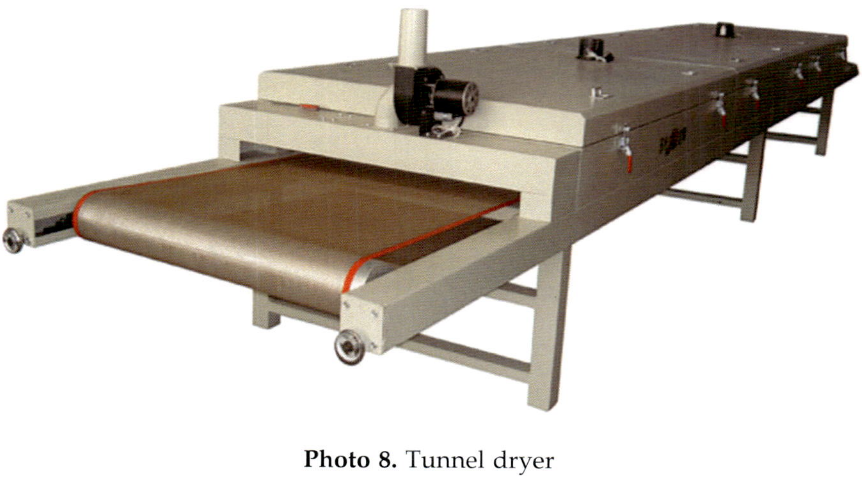

**Photo 8.** Tunnel dryer

**Photo 9.** Spray dryer for converting liquid into powder

**Photo 10.** Retort sterilizer

**Photo 11.** Juice processing plant

# CHAPTER 5

**Photo 12.** Sensory evaluation

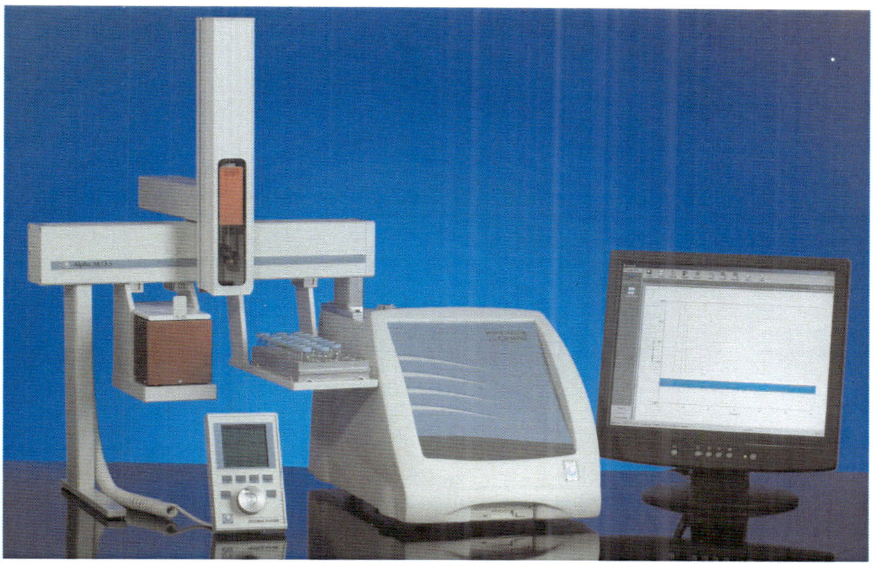

**Photo 13.** Electronic nose

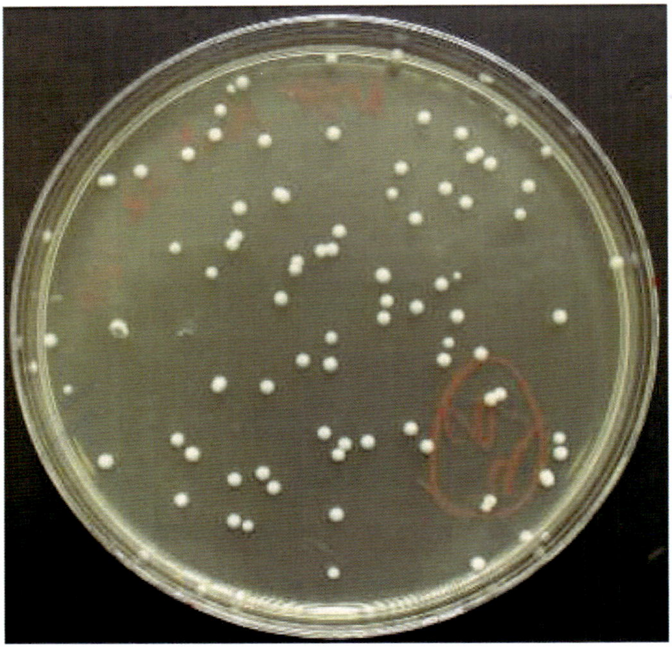

**Photo 14.** Bacterial colonies for determination of microbial count

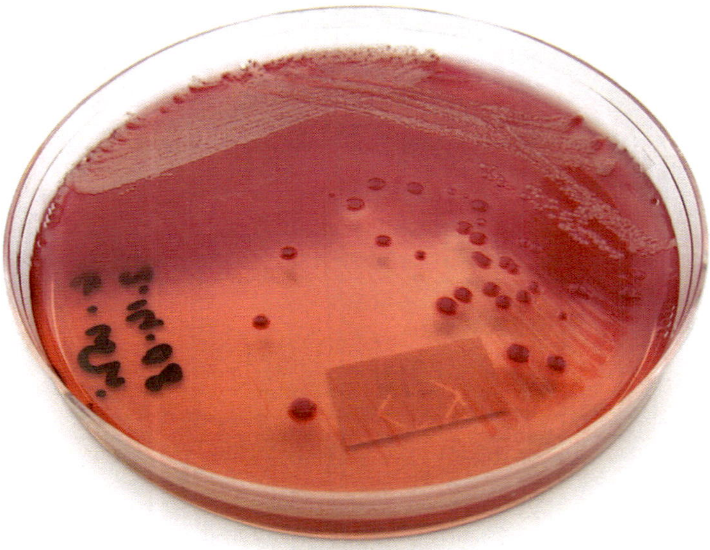

**Photo 15.** Coliform bacteria suggesting presence of pathogens

# CHAPTER 6

**Photo 16.** Powder filling machine

**Photo 17.** FFS machine for pouch packing

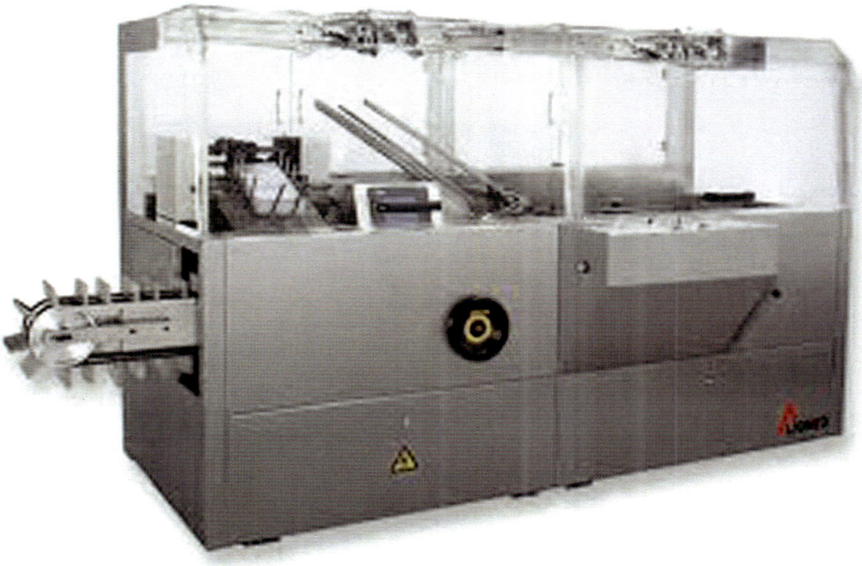

**Photo 18.** Automatic sachet cartoning machine

**Photo 19.** Aseptic liquid filler

# CHAPTER 9

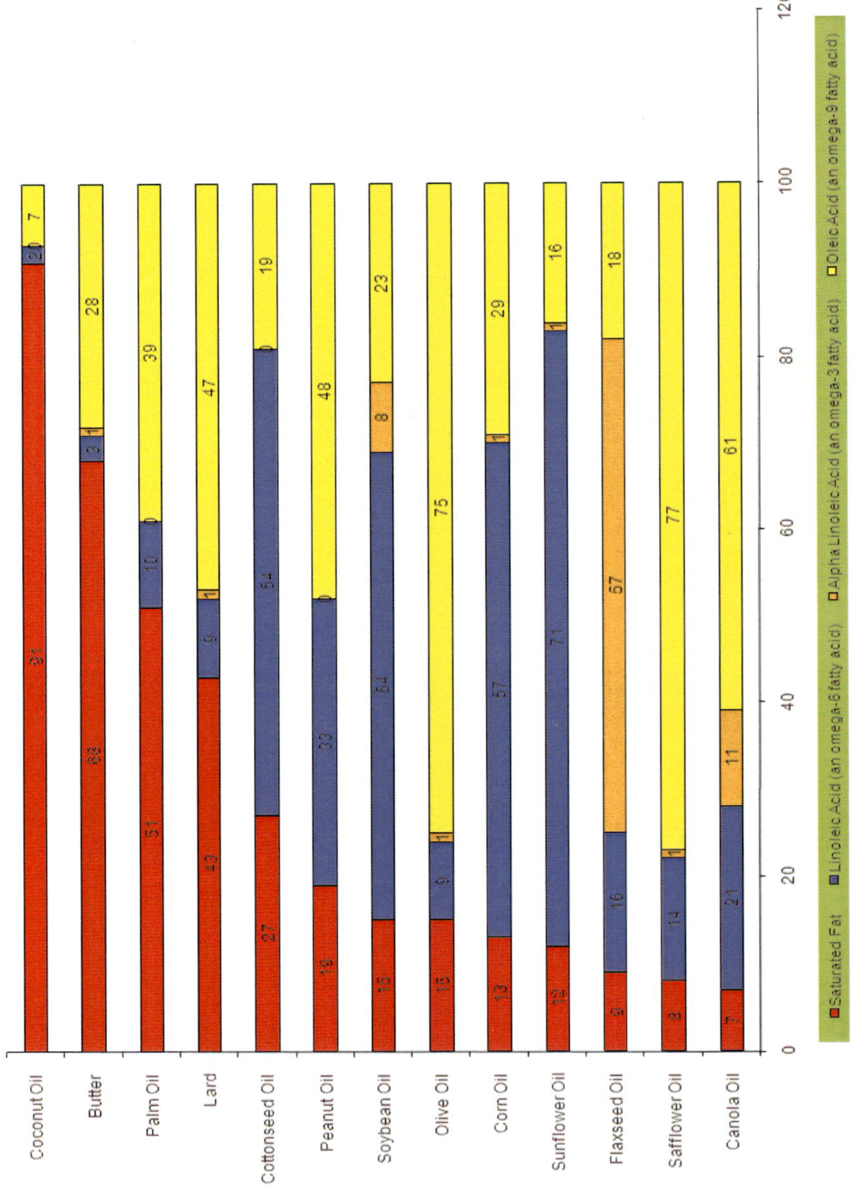


**Photo 20.** Composition of saturated and unsaturated fats in commonly used oils

# CHAPTER 11

**Photo 21.** GM brown rice rich in nutrients

**Photo 22.** GM tomatoes – Stay fresh till processing

**Photo 23.** GM corn – Used to produce ethanol, a substitute for petrol

**Photo 24.** Ethanol manufacturing plant